RESUMES  FOR
SCIENCE CAREERS

SECOND EDITION

RESUMES FOR

SCIENCE CAREERS

The Editors of McGraw-Hill

New York   Chicago   San Francisco   Lisbon   London   Madrid   Mexico City
Milan   New Delhi   San Juan   Seoul   Singapore   Sydney   Toronto

Library of Congress Cataloging-in-Publication Data

Resumes for science careers. — 2nd ed. / by the editors of McGraw-Hill.
    p.   cm.
ISBN 0-07-147619-9 (pbk. : acid-free paper)
  1. Science—Vocational guidance—Handbooks, manuals, etc.   2. Resumes
(Employment)—Handbooks, manuals, etc.   3. Applications for positions—
Handbooks, manuals, etc.   I. McGraw-Hill Companies.

Q147.R45   2007
650.14'2—dc22   2006047309

1 2 3 4 5 6 7 8 9 10 11 12 13 14 15 16 17 18 19 20 21 QPD/QPD 0 9 8 7

ISBN-13: 978-0-07-147619-5
ISBN-10:   0-07-147619-9

McGraw-Hill books are available at special quantity discounts to use as premiums and
sales promotions, or for use in corporate training programs. For more information, please
write to the Director of Special Sales, Professional Publishing, McGraw-Hill, Two Penn
Plaza, New York, NY 10121-2298. Or contact your local bookstore.

650.142
R437

This book is printed on acid-free paper.

Contents

Introduction

Your resume is a piece of paper (or an electronic document) that serves to introduce you to the people who will eventually hire you. To write a thoughtful resume, you must thoroughly assess your personality, your accomplishments, and the skills you have acquired. The act of composing and submitting a resume also requires you to carefully consider the company or individual that might hire you. What are they looking for, and how can you meet their needs? This book shows you how to organize your personal information and experience into a concise and well-written resume, so that your qualifications and potential as an employee will be understood easily and quickly by a complete stranger.

Writing the resume is just one step in what can be a daunting job-search process, but it is an important element in the chain of events that will lead you to your new position. While you are probably a talented, bright, and charming person, your resume may not reflect these qualities. A poorly written resume can get you nowhere; a well-written resume can land you an interview and potentially a job. A good resume can even lead the interviewer to ask you questions that will allow you to talk about your strengths and highlight the skills you can bring to a prospective employer. Even a person with very little experience can find a good job if he or she is assisted by a thoughtful and polished resume.

Lengthy, typewritten resumes are a thing of the past. Today, employers do not have the time or the patience for verbose documents; they look for tightly composed, straightforward, action-based resumes. Although a one-page resume is the norm, a two-page resume may be warranted if you have had extensive job experience or have changed careers and truly need the space to properly position yourself. If, after careful editing, you still need more than one page to present yourself, it's acceptable to use a second page. A crowded resume that's hard to read would be the worst of your choices.

Distilling your work experience, education, and interests into such a small space requires preparation and thought. This book takes you step-by-step through the process of crafting an effective resume that will stand out in today's competitive marketplace. It serves as a workbook and a place to write down your experiences, while also including the techniques you'll need to pull all the necessary elements together. In the following pages, you'll find many examples of resumes that are specific to your area of interest. Study them for inspiration and find what appeals to you. There are a variety of ways to organize and present your information; inside, you'll find several that will be suitable to your needs. Good luck landing the job of your dreams!

Chapter 1

The Elements of an Effective Resume

An effective resume is composed of information that employers are most interested in knowing about a prospective job applicant. This information is conveyed by a few essential elements. The following is a list of elements that are found in most resumes—some essential, some optional. Later in this chapter, we will further examine the role of each of these elements in the makeup of your resume.

- Heading
- Objective and/or Keyword Section
- Work Experience
- Education
- Honors
- Activities
- Certificates and Licenses
- Publications
- Professional Memberships
- Special Skills
- Personal Information
- References

The first step in preparing your resume is to gather information about yourself and your past accomplishments. Later you will refine this information, rewrite it using effective language, and organize it into an attractive layout. But first, let's take a look at each of these important elements individually so you can judge their appropriateness for your resume.

Heading

Although the heading may seem to be the simplest section of your resume, be careful not to take it lightly. It is the first section your prospective employer will see, and it contains the information she or he will need to contact you. At the very least, the heading must contain your name, your home address, and, of course, a phone number where you can be reached easily.

In today's high-tech world, many of us have multiple ways that we can be contacted. You may list your e-mail address if you are reasonably sure the employer makes use of this form of communication. Keep in mind, however, that others may have access to your e-mail messages if you send them from an account provided by your current company. If this is a concern, do not list your work e-mail address on your resume. If you are able to take calls at your current place of business, you should include your work number, because most employers will attempt to contact you during typical business hours.

If you have voice mail or a reliable answering machine at home or at work, list its number in the heading and make sure your greeting is professional and clear. Always include at least one phone number in your heading, even if it is a temporary number, where a prospective employer can leave a message.

You might have a dozen different ways to be contacted, but you do not need to list all of them. Confine your numbers or addresses to those that are the easiest for the prospective employer to use and the simplest for you to retrieve.

Objective

When seeking a specific career path, it is important to list a job or career objective on your resume. This statement helps employers know the direction you see yourself taking, so they can determine whether your goals are in line with those of their organization and the position available. Normally, an objective is one to two sentences long. Its contents will vary depending on your career field, goals, and personality. The objective can be specific or general, but it should always be to the point. See the sample resumes in this book for examples.

If you are planning to use this resume online, or you suspect your potential employer is likely to scan your resume, you will want to include a "keyword" in the objective. This allows a prospective employer, searching hundreds of resumes for a specific skill or position objective, to locate the keyword and find your resume. In essence, a keyword is what's "hot" in your particular field at a given time. It's a buzzword, a shorthand way of getting a particular message across at a glance. For example, if you are a lawyer, your objective might state your desire to work in the area of corporate litigation. In this case, someone searching for the keyword "corporate litigation" will pull up your resume and know that you want to plan, research, and present cases at trial on behalf of the corporation. If your objective states that you "desire a challenging position in systems design," the keyword is "systems design," an industry-specific shorthand way of saying that you want to be involved in assessing the need for, acquiring, and implementing high-technology systems. These are keywords and every industry has them, so it's becoming more and more important to include a few in your resume. (You may need to conduct additional research to make sure you know what keywords are most likely to be used in your desired industry, profession, or situation.)

There are many resume and job-search sites online. Like most things in the online world, they vary a great deal in quality. Use your discretion. If you plan to apply for jobs online or advertise your availability this way, you will want to design a scannable resume. This type of resume uses a format that can be easily scanned into a computer and added to a database. Scanning allows a prospective employer to use keywords to quickly review each applicant's experience and skills, and (in the event that there are many candidates for the job) to keep your resume for future reference.

Many people find that it is worthwhile to create two or more versions of their basic resume. You may want an intricately designed resume on high-quality paper to mail or hand out *and* a resume that is designed to be scanned into a computer and saved on a database or an online job site. You can even create a resume in ASCII text to e-mail to prospective employers. For further information, you may wish to refer to the *Guide to Internet Job Searching*, by Frances Roehm and Margaret Dikel, updated and published every other year by McGraw-Hill. This excellent book contains helpful and detailed information about formatting a resume for Internet use. To get you started, in Chapter 3 we have included a list of things to keep in mind when creating electronic resumes.

Although it is usually a good idea to include an objective, in some cases this element is not necessary. The goal of the objective statement is to provide the employer with an idea of where you see yourself going in the field. However, if you are uncertain of the exact nature of the job you seek, including an objective that is too specific could result in your not being considered for a host of perfectly acceptable positions. If you decide not to use an objective heading in your resume, you should definitely incorporate the information that would be conveyed in the objective into your cover letter.

Work Experience

Work experience is arguably the most important element of them all. Unless you are a recent graduate or former homemaker with little or no relevant work experience, your current and former positions will provide the central focus of the resume. You will want this section to be as complete and carefully constructed as possible. By thoroughly examining your work experience, you can get to the heart of your accomplishments and present them in a way that demonstrates and highlights your qualifications.

If you are just entering the workforce, your resume will probably focus on your education, but you should also include information on your work or volunteer experiences. Although you will have less information about work experience than a person who has held multiple positions or is advanced in his or her career, the amount of information is not what is most important in this section. How the information is presented and what it says about you as a worker and a person are what really count.

As you create this section of your resume, remember the need for accuracy. Include all the necessary information about each of your jobs, including your job title, dates of employment, name of your employer, city, state, responsibilities, special projects you handled, and accomplishments. Be sure to list only accomplishments for which you were directly responsible. And don't be alarmed if you haven't participated in or worked on special projects, because this section may not be relevant to certain jobs.

The most common way to list your work experience is in *reverse chronological order*. In other words, start with your most recent job and work your way backward. This way, your prospective employer sees your current (and often most important) position before considering your past employment. Your most recent position, if it's the most important in terms of responsibilities and relevance to the job for which you are applying, should also be the one that includes the most information as compared to your previous positions.

Even if the work itself seems unrelated to your proposed career path, you should list any job or experience that will help sell your talents. If you were promoted or given greater responsibilities or commendations, be sure to mention the fact.

The following worksheet is provided to help you organize your experiences in the working world. It will also serve as an excellent resource to refer to when updating your resume in the future.

WORK EXPERIENCE

Job One:

Job Title _____

Dates _____

Employer _____

City, State _____

Major Duties _____

_____

_____

_____

_____

_____

_____

_____

Special Projects _____

_____

_____

_____

Accomplishments _____

_____

_____

_____

_____

_____

Job Two:

Job Title _____

Dates _____

Employer _____

City, State _____

Major Duties _____

_____

_____

_____

_____

_____

_____

_____

Special Projects _____

_____

_____

_____

Accomplishments _____

_____

_____

_____

_____

_____

_____

_____

Job Three:

Job Title _____

Dates _____

Employer _____

City, State _____

Major Duties _____

_____

_____

_____

_____

_____

_____

Special Projects _____

_____

_____

_____

Accomplishments _____

_____

_____

_____

_____

_____

_____

_____

Job Four:

Job Title _____

Dates _____

Employer _____

City, State _____

Major Duties _____

_____

_____

_____

_____

_____

_____

Special Projects _____

_____

_____

_____

Accomplishments _____

_____

_____

_____

_____

_____

_____

Education

Education is usually the second most important element of a resume. Your educational background is often a deciding factor in an employer's decision to interview you. Highlight your accomplishments in school as much as you did those accomplishments at work. If you are looking for your first professional job, your education or life experience will be your greatest asset because your related work experience will be minimal. In this case, the education section becomes the most important means of selling yourself.

Include in this section all the degrees or certificates you have received; your major or area of concentration; all of the honors you earned; and any relevant activities you participated in, organized, or chaired. Again, list your most recent schooling first. If you have completed graduate-level work, begin with that and work your way back through your undergraduate education. If you have completed college, you generally should not list your high-school experience; do so only if you earned special honors, you had a grade point average that was much better than the norm, or this was your highest level of education.

If you have completed a large number of credit hours in a subject that may be relevant to the position you are seeking but did not obtain a degree, you may wish to list the hours or classes you completed. Keep in mind, however, that you may be asked to explain why you did not finish the program. If you are currently in school, list the degree, certificate, or license you expect to obtain and the projected date of completion.

The following worksheet will help you gather the information you need for this section of your resume.

EDUCATION

School One _____

Major or Area of Concentration _____

Degree _____

Dates _____

School Two _____

Major or Area of Concentration _____

Degree _____

Dates _____

Honors

If you include an honors section in your resume, you should highlight any awards, honors, or memberships in honorary societies that you have received. (You may also incorporate this information into your education section.) Often, the honors are academic in nature, but this section also may be used for special achievements in sports, clubs, or other school activities. Always include the name of the organization awarding the honor and the date(s) received. Use the following worksheet to help you gather your information.

HONORS

Honor One _____

Awarding Organization _____

Date(s) _____

Honor Two _____

Awarding Organization _____

Date(s) _____

Honor Three _____

Awarding Organization _____

Date(s) _____

Honor Four _____

Awarding Organization _____

Date(s) _____

Honor Five _____

Awarding Organization _____

Date(s) _____

Activities

Perhaps you have been active in different organizations or clubs; often an employer will look at such involvement as evidence of initiative, dedication, and good social skills. Examples of your ability to take a leading role in a group should be included on a resume, if you can provide them. The activities section of your resume should present neighborhood and community activities, volunteer positions, and so forth. In general, you may want to avoid listing any organization whose name indicates the race, creed, sex, age, marital status, sexual orientation, or nation of origin of its members because this could expose you to discrimination. Use the following worksheet to list the specifics of your activities.

ACTIVITIES

Organization/Activity _____

Accomplishments _____

_____

_____

Organization/Activity _____

Accomplishments _____

_____

_____

Organization/Activity _____

Accomplishments _____

_____

_____

As your work experience grows through the years, your school activities and honors will carry less weight and be emphasized less in your resume. Eventually, you will probably list only your degree and any major honors received. As time goes by, your job performance and the experience you've gained become the most important elements in your resume, which should change to reflect this.

Certificates and Licenses

If your chosen career path requires specialized training, you may already have certificates or licenses. You should list these if the job you are seeking requires them and you, of course, have acquired them. If you have applied for a license but have not yet received it, use the phrase "application pending."

License requirements vary by state. If you have moved or are planning to relocate to another state, check with that state's board or licensing agency for all licensing requirements.

Always make sure that all of the information you list is completely accurate. Locate copies of your certificates and licenses, and check the exact date and name of the accrediting agency. Use the following worksheet to organize the necessary information.

CERTIFICATES AND LICENSES

Name of License _____

Licensing Agency _____

Date Issued _____

Name of License _____

Licensing Agency _____

Date Issued _____

Name of License _____

Licensing Agency _____

Date Issued _____

Publications

Some professions strongly encourage or even require that you publish. If you have written, coauthored, or edited any books, articles, professional papers, or works of a similar nature that pertain to your field, you will definitely want to include this element. Remember to list the date of publication and the publisher's name, and specify whether you were the sole author or a coauthor. Book, magazine, or journal titles are generally italicized, while the titles of articles within a larger publication appear in quotes. (Check with your reference librarian for more about the appropriate way to present this information.) For scientific or research papers, you will need to give the date, place, and audience to whom the paper was presented.

Use the following worksheet to help you gather the necessary information about your publications.

PUBLICATIONS

Title and Type (Note, Article, etc.) _____

Title of Publication (Journal, Book, etc.) _____

Publisher _____

Date Published _____

Title and Type (Note, Article, etc.) _____

Title of Publication (Journal, Book, etc.) _____

Publisher _____

Date Published _____

Title and Type (Note, Article, etc.) _____

Title of Publication (Journal, Book, etc.) _____

Publisher _____

Date Published _____

Professional Memberships

Another potential element in your resume is a section listing professional memberships. Use this section to describe your involvement in professional associations, unions, and similar organizations. It is to your advantage to list any professional memberships that pertain to the job you are seeking. Many employers see your membership as representative of your desire to stay up-to-date and connected in your field. Include the dates of your involvement and whether you took part in any special activities or held any offices within the organization. Use the following worksheet to organize your information.

PROFESSIONAL MEMBERSHIPS

Name of Organization _____

Office(s) Held_____

Activities _____

Dates _____

Name of Organization _____

Office(s) Held_____

Activities _____

Dates _____

Name of Organization _____

Office(s) Held_____

Activities _____

Dates _____

Name of Organization _____

Office(s) Held_____

Activities _____

Dates _____

Special Skills

The special skills section of your resume is the place to mention any special abilities you have that relate to the job you are seeking. You can use this element to present certain talents or experiences that are not necessarily a part of your education or work experience. Common examples include fluency in a foreign language, extensive travel abroad, or knowledge of a particular computer application. "Special skills" can encompass a wide range of talents, and this section can be used creatively. However, for each skill you list, you should be able to describe how it would be a direct asset in the type of work you're seeking because employers may ask just that in an interview. If you can't think of a way to do this, it may be extraneous information.

Personal Information

Some people include personal information on their resumes. This is generally not recommended, but you might wish to include it if you think that something in your personal life, such as a hobby or talent, has some bearing on the position you are seeking. This type of information is often referred to at the beginning of an interview, when it may be used as an icebreaker. Of course, personal information regarding your age, marital status, race, religion, or sexual orientation should never appear on your resume as personal information. It should be given only in the context of memberships and activities, and only when doing so would not expose you to discrimination.

References

References are not usually given on the resume itself, but a prospective employer needs to know that you have references who may be contacted if necessary. All you need to include is a single sentence at the end of the resume: "References are available upon request," or even simply, "References available." Have a reference list ready—your interviewer may ask to see it! Contact each person on the list ahead of time to see whether it is all right for you to use him or her as a reference. This way, the person has a chance to think about what to say *before* the call occurs. This helps ensure that you will obtain the best reference possible.

Chapter 2

Writing Your Resume

Now that you have gathered the information for each section of your resume, it's time to write it out in a way that will get the attention of the reviewer—hopefully, your future employer! The language you use in your resume will affect its success, so you must be careful and conscientious. Translate the facts you have gathered into the active, precise language of resume writing. You will be aiming for a resume that keeps the reader's interest and highlights your accomplishments in a concise and effective way.

Resume writing is unlike any other form of writing. Although your seventh-grade composition teacher would not approve, the rules of punctuation and sentence building are often completely ignored. Instead, you should try for a functional, direct writing style that focuses on the use of verbs and other words that imply action on your part. Writing with action words and strong verbs characterizes you to potential employers as an energetic, active person, someone who completes tasks and achieves results from his or her work. Resumes that do not make use of action words can sound passive and stale. These resumes are not effective and do not get the attention of any employer, no matter how qualified the applicant. Choose words that display your strengths and demonstrate your initiative. The following list of commonly used verbs will help you create a strong resume:

administered	assembled
advised	assumed responsibility
analyzed	billed
arranged	built

carried out	inspected
channeled	interviewed
collected	introduced
communicated	invented
compiled	maintained
completed	managed
conducted	met with
contacted	motivated
contracted	negotiated
coordinated	operated
counseled	orchestrated
created	ordered
cut	organized
designed	oversaw
determined	performed
developed	planned
directed	prepared
dispatched	presented
distributed	produced
documented	programmed
edited	published
established	purchased
expanded	recommended
functioned as	recorded
gathered	reduced
handled	referred
hired	represented
implemented	researched
improved	reviewed

saved	supervised
screened	taught
served as	tested
served on	trained
sold	typed
suggested	wrote

Let's look at two examples that differ only in their writing style. The first resume section is ineffective because it does not use action words to accent the applicant's work experiences.

WORK EXPERIENCE
Regional Sales Manager

Manager of sales representatives from seven states. Manager of twelve food chain accounts in the East. In charge of the sales force's planned selling toward specific goals. Supervisor and trainer of new sales representatives. Consulting for customers in the areas of inventory management and quality control.

Special Projects: Coordinator and sponsor of annual Food Industry Seminar.

Accomplishments: Monthly regional volume went up 25 percent during my tenure while, at the same time, a proper sales/cost ratio was maintained. Customer-company relations were improved.

In the following paragraph, we have rewritten the same section using action words. Notice how the tone has changed. It now sounds stronger and more active. This person accomplished goals and really *did* things.

WORK EXPERIENCE
Regional Sales Manager

Managed sales representatives from seven states. Oversaw twelve food chain accounts in the eastern United States. Directed the sales force in planned selling toward specific goals. Supervised and trained new sales representatives. Counseled customers in the areas of inventory management and quality control. Coordinated and sponsored the annual Food Industry Seminar. Increased monthly regional volume by 25 percent and helped to improve customer-company relations during my tenure.

One helpful way to construct the work experience section is to make use of your actual job descriptions—the written duties and expectations your employers have for a person in your current or former position. Job descriptions are rarely written in proper resume language, so you will have to rework them, but they do include much of the information necessary to create this section of your resume. If you have access to job descriptions for your former positions, you can use the details to construct an action-oriented paragraph. Often, your human resources department can provide a job description for your current position.

The following is an example of a typical human resources job description, followed by a rewritten version of the same description employing action words and specific details about the job. Again, pay attention to the style of writing instead of the content, as the details of your own experience will be unique.

WORK EXPERIENCE
Public Administrator I

Responsibilities: Coordinate and direct public services to meet the needs of the nation, state, or community. Analyze problems; work with special committees and public agencies; recommend solutions to governing bodies.

Aptitudes and Skills: Ability to relate to and communicate with people; solve complex problems through analysis; plan, organize, and implement policies and programs. Knowledge of political systems, financial management, personnel administration, program evaluation, and organizational theory.

WORK EXPERIENCE
Public Administrator I

Wrote pamphlets and conducted discussion groups to inform citizens of legislative processes and consumer issues. Organized and supervised 25 interviewers. Trained interviewers in effective communication skills.

After you have written out your resume, you are ready to begin the next important step: assembly and layout.

Chapter 3

Assembly and Layout

At this point, you've gathered all the necessary information for your resume and rewritten it in language that will impress your potential employers. Your next step is to assemble the sections in a logical order and lay them out on the page neatly and attractively to achieve the desired effect: getting the interview.

Assembly

The order of the elements in a resume makes a difference in its overall effect. Clearly, you would not want to bury your name and address somewhere in the middle of the resume. Nor would you want to lead with a less important section, such as special skills. Put the elements in an order that stresses your most important accomplishments and the things that will be most appealing to your potential employer. For example, if you are new to the workforce, you will want the reviewer to read about your education and life skills before any part-time jobs you may have held for short durations. On the other hand, if you have been gainfully employed for several years and currently hold an important position in your company, you should list your work accomplishments ahead of your educational information, which has become less pertinent with time.

Certain things should always be included in your resume, but others are optional. The following list shows you which are which. You might want to use it as a checklist to be certain that you have included all of the necessary information.

Essential	**Optional**
Name	Cellular Phone Number
Address	Pager Number
Phone Number	E-Mail Address or Website Address
Work Experience	Voice Mail Number
Education	Job Objective
References Phrase	Honors
	Special Skills
	Publications
	Professional Memberships
	Activities
	Certificates and Licenses
	Personal Information
	Graphics
	Photograph

Your choice of optional sections depends on your own background and employment needs. Always use information that will put you in a favorable light—unless it's absolutely essential, avoid anything that will prompt the interviewer to ask questions about your weaknesses or something else that could be unflattering. Make sure your information is accurate and truthful. If your honors are impressive, include them in the resume. If your activities in school demonstrate talents that are necessary for the job you are seeking, allow space for a section on activities. If you are applying for a position that requires ornamental illustration, you may want to include border illustrations or graphics that demonstrate your talents in this area. If you are answering an advertisement for a job that requires certain physical traits, a photo of yourself might be appropriate. A person applying for a job as a computer programmer would *not* include a photo as part of his or her resume. Each resume is unique, just as each person is unique.

Types of Resumes

So far we have focused on the most common type of resume—the *reverse chronological* resume—in which your most recent job is listed first. This is the type of resume usually preferred by those who have to read a large number of resumes, and it is by far the most popular and widely circulated. However, this style of presentation may not be the most effective way to highlight *your* skills and accomplishments.

For example, if you are reentering the workforce after many years or are trying to change career fields, the *functional* resume may work best. This type of resume puts the focus on your achievements instead of the sequence of your work history. In the functional resume, your experience is presented through your general accomplishments and the skills you have developed in your working life.

A functional resume is assembled from the same information you gathered in Chapter 1. The main difference lies in how you organize the information. Essentially, the work experience section is divided in two, with your job duties and accomplishments constituting one section and your employers' names, cities, and states; your positions; and the dates employed making up the other. Place the first section near the top of your resume, just below your job objective (if used), and call it *Accomplishments* or *Achievements*. The second section, containing the bare essentials of your work history, should come after the accomplishments section and can be called *Employment History*, since it is a chronological overview of your former jobs.

The other sections of your resume remain the same. The work experience section is the only one affected in the functional format. By placing the section that focuses on your achievements at the beginning, you draw attention to these achievements. This puts less emphasis on where you worked and when, and more on what you did and what you are capable of doing.

If you are changing careers, the emphasis on skills and achievements is important. The identities of previous employers (who aren't part of your new career field) need to be downplayed. A functional resume can help accomplish this task. If you are reentering the workforce after a long absence, a functional resume is the obvious choice. And if you lack full-time work experience, you will need to draw attention away from this fact and put the focus on your skills and abilities. You may need to highlight your volunteer activities and part-time work. Education may also play a more important role in your resume.

The type of resume that is right for you will depend on your personal circumstances. It may be helpful to create both types and then compare them. Which one presents you in the best light? Examples of both types of resumes are included in this book. Use the sample resumes in Chapter 5 to help you decide on the content, presentation, and look of your own resume.

Resume or Curriculum Vitae?

A curriculum vitae (CV) is a longer, more detailed synopsis of your professional history that generally runs three or more pages in length. It includes a summary of your educational and academic background as well as teaching and research experience, publications, presentations, awards, honors, affiliations, and other details. Because the purpose of the CV is different from that of the resume, many of the rules we've discussed thus far involving style and length do not apply.

A curriculum vitae is used primarily for admissions applications to graduate or professional schools, independent consulting in a variety of settings, proposals for fellowships or grants, or applications for positions in academia. As with a resume, you may need different versions of a CV for different types of positions. You should only send a CV when one is specifically requested by an employer or institution.

Like a resume, your CV should include your name, contact information, education, skills, and experience. In addition to the basics, a CV includes research and teaching experience, publications, grants and fellowships, professional associations and licenses, awards, and other information relevant to the position for which you are applying. You can follow the advice presented thus far to gather and organize your personal information.

Special Tips for Electronic Resumes

Because there are many details to consider in writing a resume that will be posted or transmitted on the Internet, or one that will be scanned into a computer when it is received, we suggest that you refer to the *Guide to Internet Job Searching*, by Frances Roehm and Margaret Dikel, as previously mentioned. However, here are some brief, general guidelines to follow if you expect your resume to be scanned into a computer.

- Use standard fonts in which none of the letters touch.

- Keep in mind that underlining, italics, and fancy scripts may not scan well.

- Use boldface and capitalization to set off elements. Again, make sure letters don't touch. Leave at least a quarter inch between lines of type.

- Keep information and elements at the left margin. Centering, columns, and even indenting may change when the resume is optically scanned.

- Do not use any lines, boxes, or graphics.

- Place the most important information at the top of the first page. If you use two pages, put "Page 1 of 2" at the bottom of the first page and put your name and "Page 2 of 2" at the top of the second page.

- List each telephone number on its own line in the header.

- Use multiple keywords or synonyms for what you do to make sure your qualifications will be picked up if a prospective employer is searching for them. Use nouns that are keywords for your profession.

- Be descriptive in your titles. For example, don't just use "assistant"; use "legal office assistant."

- Make sure the contrast between print and paper is good. Use a high-quality laser printer and white or very light colored 8½-by-11-inch paper.

- Mail a high-quality laser print or an excellent copy. Do not fold or use staples, as this might interfere with scanning. You may, however, use paper clips.

In addition to creating a resume that works well for scanning, you may want to have a resume that can be e-mailed to reviewers. Because you may not know what word processing application the recipient uses, the best format to use is ASCII text. (ASCII stands for "American Standard Code for Information Interchange.") It allows people with very different software platforms to exchange and understand information. (E-mail operates on this principle.) ASCII is a simple, text-only language, which means you can include only simple text. There can be no use of boldface, italics, or even paragraph indentations.

To create an ASCII resume, just use your normal word processing program; when finished, save it as a "text only" document. You will find this option under the "save" or "save as" command. Here is a list of things to *avoid* when crafting your electronic resume:

- Tabs. Use your space bar. Tabs will not work.

- Any special characters, such as mathematical symbols.

- Word wrap. Use hard returns (the return key) to make line breaks.

- Centering or other formatting. Align everything at the left margin.

- Bold or italic fonts. Everything will be converted to plain text when you save the file as a "text only" document.

Check carefully for any mistakes before you save the document as a text file. Spellcheck and proofread it several times; then ask someone with a keen eye to go over it again for you. Remember: the key is to keep it simple. Any attempt to make this resume pretty or decorative may result in a resume that is confusing and hard to read. After you have saved the document, you can cut and paste it into an e-mail or onto a website.

Layout for a Paper Resume

A great deal of care—and much more formatting—is necessary to achieve an attractive layout for your paper resume. There is no single appropriate layout that applies to every resume, but there are a few basic rules to follow in putting your resume on paper:

- Leave a comfortable margin on the sides, top, and bottom of the page (usually one to one and a half inches).

- Use appropriate spacing between the sections (two to three line spaces are usually adequate).

- Be consistent in the *type* of headings you use for different sections of your resume. For example, if you capitalize the heading EMPLOYMENT HISTORY, don't use initial capitals and underlining for a section of equal importance, such as Education.

- Do not use more than one font in your resume. Stay consistent by choosing a font that is fairly standard and easy to read, and don't change it for different sections. Beware of the tendency to try to make your resume original by choosing fancy type styles; your resume may end up looking unprofessional instead of creative. Unless you are in a very creative and artistic field, you should almost always stick with tried-and-true type styles like Times New Roman and Palatino, which are often used in business writing. In the area of resume styles, conservative is usually the best way to go.

CHRONOLOGICAL RESUME

JUAN CASTILLO

1088 S. Hampton Rd. • Baltimore, MD 21275 • Juan.Castillo@xxx.com • (410) 555-2896

EXPERIENCE

September 2002 to Present, Urban Planning Consultant
City of Baltimore, Department of Community Development

• Consult with city and county governments on community development.
• Inspect sites for new and expanding communities.
• Ensure compliance with municipal codes on construction projects currently
  underway.
• Contribute to long-range planning committee reports.
• Advise government officials on inner-city redevelopment and historic preservation
  projects.

August 1999 to September 2002, Public Health Inspector
State of Maryland, Maryland Public Safety Council

• Collected and analyzed samples to assess air quality and water pollution.
• Inspected suspected sites of pollution and issued status reports and
  recommendations.

May 1996 to September 1999, Environmental Scientist
Bureau of Land Management, State of Maine

• Responsible for stream and timber management.
• Created topographical maps.

EDUCATION

B.S. University of Baltimore, 1996
Double major in Environmental Studies and Urban Planning

References on request.

FUNCTIONAL RESUME

Sylvia K. Warren, D.V.M.
232 Aston Place, #205
Boston, MA 02129
s.warren@xxx.com
(617) 555-2716

Objective
Full-time veterinarian position in animal hospital or clinic with opportunity for eventual supervisory responsibilities.

Experience
- Extensive experience in private small-animal practice providing both routine and emergency care.
- Strong diagnostic and surgical skills.
- Excellent recovery rate.
- Strong interpersonal and communications skills.
- Ability to manage staff, creating an efficient workflow.

Employers
Martindale Veterinary Clinic, Boston, MA
June 2004 to Present

TDK Veterinary Medical Center, Baltimore, MD
April 2001 to June 2004

Credentials
- D.V.M., University of Massachusetts, 2001
- Licensed D.V.M., Maryland and Massachusetts
- Member, American Veterinary Medical Association

References available.

- Always try to fit your resume on one page. If you are having trouble with this, you may be trying to say too much. Edit out any repetitive or unnecessary information, and shorten descriptions of earlier jobs where possible. Ask a friend you trust for feedback on what seems unnecessary or unimportant. For example, you may have included too many optional sections. Today, with the prevalence of the personal computer as a tool, there is no excuse for a poorly laid out resume. Experiment with variations until you are pleased with the result.

Remember that a resume is not an autobiography. Too much information will only get in the way. The more compact your resume, the easier it will be to review. If a person who is swamped with resumes looks at yours, catches the main points, and then calls you for an interview to fill in some of the details, your resume has already accomplished its task. A clear and concise resume makes for a happy reader and a good impression.

There are times when, despite extensive editing, the resume simply cannot fit on one page. In this case, the resume should be laid out on two pages in such a way that neither clarity nor appearance is compromised. Each page of a two-page resume should be marked clearly: the first should indicate "Page 1 of 2," and the second should include your name and the page number, for example, "Julia Ramirez—Page 2 of 2." The pages should then be paper-clipped together. You may use a smaller type size (in the same font as the body of your resume) for the page numbers. Place them at the bottom of page one and the top of page two. Again, spend the time now to experiment with the layout until you find one that looks good to you.

Always show your final layout to other people and ask them what they like or dislike about it, and what impresses them most when they read your resume. Make sure that their responses are the same as what you want to elicit from your prospective employer. If they aren't the same, you should continue to make changes until the necessary information is emphasized.

Proofreading

After you have finished typing the master copy of your resume and before you have it copied or printed, thoroughly check it for typing and spelling errors. Do not place all your trust in your computer's spellcheck function. Use an old editing trick and read the whole resume backward—start at the end and read it right to left and bottom to top. This can help you see the small errors or inconsistencies that are easy to overlook. Take time to do it right because a single error on a document this important can cause the reader to judge your attention to detail in a harsh light.

Have several people look at the finished resume just in case you've missed an error. Don't try to take a shortcut; not having an unbiased set of eyes examine your resume now could mean embarrassment later. Even experienced editors can easily overlook their own errors. Be thorough and conscientious with your proofreading so your first impression is a perfect one.

We have included the following rules of capitalization and punctuation to assist you in the final stage of creating your resume. Remember that resumes often require use of a shorthand style of writing that may include sentences without periods and other stylistic choices that break the standard rules of grammar. Be consistent in each section and throughout the whole resume with your choices.

RULES OF CAPITALIZATION

- Capitalize proper nouns, such as names of schools, colleges, and universities; names of companies; and brand names of products.

- Capitalize major words in the names and titles of books, tests, and articles that appear in the body of your resume.

- Capitalize words in major section headings of your resume.

- Do not capitalize words just because they seem important.

- When in doubt, consult a style manual such as *Words into Type* (Prentice Hall) or *The Chicago Manual of Style* (The University of Chicago Press). Your local library can help you locate these and other reference books. Many computer programs also have grammar help sections.

RULES OF PUNCTUATION

- Use commas to separate words in a series.

- Use a semicolon to separate series of words that already include commas within the series. (For an example, see the first rule of capitalization.)

- Use a semicolon to separate independent clauses that are not joined by a conjunction.

- Use a period to end a sentence.

- Use a colon to show that examples or details follow that will expand or amplify the preceding phrase.

- Avoid the use of dashes.

- Avoid the use of brackets.

- If you use any punctuation in an unusual way in your resume, be consistent in its use.

- Whenever you are uncertain, consult a style manual.

Putting Your Resume in Print

You will need to buy high-quality paper for your printer before you print your finished resume. Regular office paper is not good enough for resumes; the reviewer will probably think it looks flimsy and cheap. Go to an office supply store or copy shop and select a high-quality bond paper that will make a good first impression. Select colors like white, off-white, or possibly a light gray. In some industries, a pastel may be acceptable, but be sure the color and feel of the paper make a subtle, positive statement about you. Nothing in the choice of paper should be loud or unprofessional.

If your computer printer does not reproduce your resume properly and produces smudged or stuttered type, either ask to borrow a friend's or take your disk (or a clean original) to a printer or copy shop for high-quality copying. If you anticipate needing a large number of copies, taking your resume to a copy shop or a printer is probably the best choice.

Hold a sheet of your unprinted bond paper up to the light. If it has a watermark, you will want to point this out to the person helping you with copies; the printing should be done so that the reader can read the print and see the watermark the right way up. Check each copy for smudges or streaks. This is the time to be a perfectionist—the results of your careful preparation will be well worth it.

Chapter 4

The Cover Letter

Once your resume has been assembled, laid out, and printed to your satisfaction, the next and final step before distribution is to write your cover letter. Though there may be instances where you deliver your resume in person, you will usually send it through the mail or online. Resumes sent through the mail always need an accompanying letter that briefly introduces you and your resume. The purpose of the cover letter is to get a potential employer to read your resume, just as the purpose of the resume is to get that same potential employer to call you for an interview.

Like your resume, your cover letter should be clean, neat, and direct. A cover letter usually includes the following information:

1. Your name and address (unless it already appears on your personal letterhead) and your phone number(s); see item 7.

2. The date.

3. The name and address of the person and company to whom you are sending your resume.

4. The salutation ("Dear Mr." or "Dear Ms." followed by the person's last name, or "To Whom It May Concern" if you are answering a blind ad).

5. An opening paragraph explaining why you are writing (for example, in response to an ad, as a follow-up to a previous meeting, at the suggestion of someone you both know) and indicating that you are interested in whatever job is being offered.

6. One or more paragraphs that tell why you want to work for the company and what qualifications and experiences you can bring to the position. This is a good place to mention some detail about

that particular company that makes you want to work for them; this shows that you have done some research before applying.

7. A final paragraph that closes the letter and invites the reviewer to contact you for an interview. This can be a good place to tell the potential employer which method would be best to use when contacting you. Be sure to give the correct phone number and a good time to reach you, if that is important. You may mention here that your references are available upon request.

8. The closing ("Sincerely" or "Yours truly") followed by your signature in a dark ink, with your name typed under it.

Your cover letter should include all of this information and be no longer than one page in length. The language used should be polite, businesslike, and to the point. Don't attempt to tell your life story in the cover letter; a long and cluttered letter will serve only to annoy the reader. Remember that you need to mention only a few of your accomplishments and skills in the cover letter. The rest of your information is available in your resume. If your cover letter is a success, your resume will be read and all pertinent information reviewed by your prospective employer.

Producing the Cover Letter

Cover letters should always be individualized because they are always written to specific individuals and companies. Never use a form letter for your cover letter or copy it as you would a resume. Each cover letter should be unique, and as personal and lively as possible. (Of course, once you have written and rewritten your first cover letter until you are satisfied with it, you can certainly use similar wording in subsequent letters. You may want to save a template on your computer for future reference.) Keep a hard copy of each cover letter so you know exactly what you wrote in each one.

There are sample cover letters in Chapter 6. Use them as models or for ideas of how to assemble and lay out your own cover letters. Remember that every letter is unique and depends on the particular circumstances of the individual writing it and the job for which he or she is applying.

After you have written your cover letter, proofread it as thoroughly as you did your resume. Again, spelling or punctuation errors are a sure sign of carelessness, and you don't want that to be a part of your first impression on a prospective employer. This is no time to trust your spellcheck function. Even after going through a spelling and grammar check, your cover letter should be carefully proofread by at least one other person.

Print the cover letter on the same quality bond paper you used for your resume. Remember to sign it, using a good dark-ink pen. Handle the letter and resume carefully to avoid smudging or wrinkling, and mail them together in an appropriately sized envelope. Many stores sell matching envelopes to coordinate with your choice of bond paper.

Keep an accurate record of all resumes you send out and the results of each mailing. This record can be kept on your computer, in a calendar or notebook, or on file cards. Knowing when a resume is likely to have been received will keep you on track as you make follow-up phone calls.

About a week after mailing resumes and cover letters to potential employers, contact them by telephone. Confirm that your resume arrived and ask whether an interview might be possible. Be sure to record the name of the person you spoke to and any other information you gleaned from the conversation. It is wise to treat the person answering the phone with a great deal of respect; sometimes the assistant or receptionist has the ear of the person doing the hiring.

You should make a great impression with the strong, straightforward resume and personalized cover letter you have just created. We wish you every success in securing the career of your dreams!

Chapter 5

Sample Resumes

This chapter contains dozens of sample resumes for people pursuing a wide variety of jobs and careers.

There are many different styles of resumes in terms of graphic layout and presentation of information. These samples also represent people with varying amounts of education and experience. Use these samples to model your own resume after. Choose one resume, or borrow elements from several different resumes to help you construct your own.

Carolyn Haynes

826 Morris Road
East Lansing, MI 48826
Home: 517-555-1810
Cell: 517-555-3812

GOAL

Full-time assistant research scientist

JOB HISTORY

IGN FOODSERVICE, INC.
Quality Control Tester, 8/04 to Present

• Sample food products to ensure compliance with company and FDA standards.

• Use thermometers, scales, and chemical analyzers to test random samples.

• Report any substandard samples to quality control inspector.

GOURMET BASKETS, INC.
Packager, 6/03 to 8/04

• Assisted gourmet food distributor at retail store and in preparing inventory for mail-order business.

• Inspected and washed fresh produce.

• Packaged and labeled gift baskets while monitoring for superior quality.

EDUCATION

Graduate, East Lansing High, 2003

• Active in Junior Achievement Program

• Honor Roll, junior and senior year

REFERENCES AVAILABLE

SUSAN WRIGHT

657 King Court
Atlanta, Georgia 30356
Susan.Wright@xxx.com
404-555-4959

EXPERIENCE

7/04 to 9/06
Quality Control Engineer, Powell Metallurgical

- Responsible for project management of meteorological and particulate monitoring programs for mining operations.
- Directed collection and processing of data sets.
- Ensured company compliance with EPA and state guidelines for pollution control.

5/04 to 7/04
Field Researcher, Emerson Water Research Center

- Responsible for field research related to water quality control projects.
- Sampled stream water and monitored nutrient loads, water level, and insect species present.
- Input data into spreadsheets for analysis.

EDUCATION

B. S., Environmental Engineering
University of Florida, Gainesville
May 2004

Undergraduate courses included Pollution Control Design, Wastewater System Design, and Atmospheric Dispersion Modeling.

MEMBERSHIPS

- Member, National Air and Waste Management Association
- Member, Women in Environmental Science

CERTIFICATION

Mine Safety and Health Administration Certification, U.S. Department of Labor

References available upon request.

Omar Hasak

5422 Dalton Road ■ Chicago, IL 60648
o.hasak@xxx.com ■ 773-555-4949

■ ■ ■

OBJECTIVE

Professional opportunity with an environmental firm that requires specialized knowledge in hazardous waste disposal, wastewater treatment programs, industrial permits, and land applications.

EXPERIENCE

Environmental Specialist
Illinois Bureau of Research Management

2/03 to Present
Director, Emergency Resource Team

■ Direct the removal and disposal of toxic wastes.

■ Assess damage and develop cleanup strategy.

■ Solicit and review contractor bids.

■ Develop and enforce safety standards in conjunction with legal and environmental experts.

8/00 to 2/03
Documentation Specialist, Water Management Division

■ Reviewed and modified facilities-planning documents and project costs.

■ Assisted in establishing construction budgets and schedules.

■ Reviewed industrial permit requests and land applications for accuracy and completeness.

CREDENTIALS

B.S., Natural Resources Management, Northern Illinois University, 2000
Member, Institute of Hazardous Materials Management

REFERENCES

Available

CARLOS DE LA PAZ

9916 Pasco Drive

Pullman, WA 99164

(509) 555-5616

GOAL:

Position as Vector Control Supervisor

JOB EXPERIENCE:

8/04 to Present
Vector Control Worker II, State of Washington

6/02 to 8/04
Vector Control Worker I, State of Washington

HIGHLIGHTS:

- Pest control experience: chemical treatment and/or fumigation of parks, agricultural fields, landscaped areas
- Current director of mosquito abatement program
- Comfortable operating power sprayers, trucks, spreaders, and tractors
- Valid license and clean driving record

EDUCATION:

Coursework, Integrated Pest Management Program, Washington State University
2003 to 2004, 12 credit hours completed

Graduate, Pullman High School, 2002

AFFILIATIONS:

Union member, United Public Workers

References Available

Miles Edmonds

5328 Jefferson Street

St. Louis, MO 63119

m.edmonds@xxx.com

314-555-0598 - Home

314-555-0597 - Cell

Environmental Services Consultant—Professional Air Quality Control

SERVICES

- Air Testing Services
- Air Systems Decontamination
- Systems Maintenance and Repair
- Commercial and Residential Building Inspection

CREDENTIALS

B.S. in Environmental Science, University of Illinois, 2004
Certified Building Inspector, State of Missouri #A67092-48

JOB HISTORY

2004 to Present
Air Quality Electronics Technician, State of Missouri

- Set up, calibrate, maintain, and repair air quality control equipment, including spectrophotometer, carbon monoxide analyzer, and nitric oxide-nitrogen dioxide analyzer.
- Work at central lab and sampling sites statewide.
- Enter findings into database for evaluation.

JOB HISTORY *continued*

2000 to 2004, summers
Maintenance Technician, PCA Heating and Air Conditioning Inc.

- Maintained and repaired residential and commercial systems.

- Installed pulse gas, electric, and oil furnaces and high-efficiency air conditioners.

- Knowledgeable of and worked in compliance with all Missouri state safety laws.

1998 to 2000
Assistant Building Inspector, City of St. Louis

- Inspected commercial and residential structures to verify compliance with city fire, safety, and building codes.

- Issued verbal and written inspection reports to chief inspector.

REFERENCES AVAILABLE

Kevin Donaldson

4028 Carson Road
New Haven, CT 06510
K.Donaldson@xxx.com
203-555-2432

Background

Experienced educator with state and national teaching certification along with a degree in biology. Current objective is full-time position with a public or private secondary school teaching Life Sciences, Chemistry, or Physics. Strong and current computer skills, provide online tutoring and homework assistance. Proven record of motivating students and increasing test scores.

Employers

Parkland Academy
Head of Science Department
2000 - Present

Central High School
Science Instructor
1993 - 2000

Education

M.A., University of Maryland, 1993
Major: Education

Secondary Teaching Certification, National Board for Professional Teaching Standards, 1993

Connecticut State Teaching License, 1993

B.S., Wheaton College, 1991
Major: Biology

References

Available

Jacob Harvey

486 Carmel Road ❖ Anaheim, California 92803
(714) 555-6976 ❖ j.harvey@xxx.com

❖ Senior Zookeeper, Anaheim Children's Zoo.

❖ Animal behaviorist with research experience.

❖ Competent in all phases of animal care.

❖ Excellent communications skills.

❖ Successful record of personnel management.

Job History

❖ *Senior Zookeeper, Anaheim Children's Zoo*
6/01 to Present

- Direct all aspects of the children's zoo.
- Responsible for staff of five.
- Supervise care of all animals and maintenance of exhibits.
- Work with zoo director to develop educational programming and special events.

❖ *Zookeeper, Primate House, Anaheim Children's Zoo*
4/96 to 6/01

- Responsible for direct care and feeding of primates and maintenance of exhibit area.
- Assisted senior animal behaviorist with ongoing study of maternal infant bonding in primates.

❖ *Veterinary Assistant, Meadows Veterinary Clinic*
3/94 to 1/96

- Part-time assistant to veterinarian with small animal practice.
- Assisted with care and feeding of ill animals.
- Assisted veterinarian with routine exams.

Education/Training

B.S., University of Wisconsin, Madison, January 1996

Biology major with minor in Psychology and coursework in Animal Psychology

Anaheim Zoo Internship Program, completed April 1996

❖ *References Available*

KEVIN HUTCHINS

9618 Bishop Street
Lihue, HI 96766
kevin.hutchins@xxx.net
(808) 555-6712 Work
(808) 555-9836 Home

EXPERIENCE

Owner, Paradise Pest Control, 9/04 to Present

Provide pest control services to residential, commercial, and industrial clients. Services include general pest control, termite inspection, ground termite control, tent fumigation, preconstruction treatment, and escrow clearance.

Exterminator, Pacific Exterminators, 6/02 to 9/04

Duties included termite inspection, ground termite control, and tent fumigation.

Pest Control Worker, County of Kauai, 6/01 to 6/02

Duties included chemical treatment of county land to reduce rodent and mosquito populations and control weed growth. Mixed pesticides and loaded power sprayers.

CREDENTIALS

P.C.O. License #725
Member, Hawaii Pest Control Association
Graduate, Kapa'a High School, 2001

References Available

Lilah Wapau

816 Bay Beach Road
Melbourne, FL 32902
(321) 555-2974

❦ Experience

5/05 to Present
Agricultural Scientist, State of Florida

- Work in conjunction with the state and local departments of agriculture and economic development to manage agricultural crops statewide.
- Fieldwork involves conducting soil surveys, analyzing fertilizers, tillage practices, and crop rotation.
- Prepare written reports on findings.

4/00 to 5/05
Research Associate, Florida State University

- Researched frost tolerance in citrus crops.
- Assisted with planting, harvesting, and analyzing and documenting crop conditions.
- Prepared progress reports and statistical data.

❦ Accomplishments

- Current consultant to Pacific Botanical Gardens.
- Working to develop pest-resistant products to enable reduced use of aerosol pesticides.
- Appointed to direct statewide research on soil erosion.

❦ Education

B.S., Agronomy, January 2000
Florida State University, Tallahassee

References on request.

ALICIA ALVEREZ

Home   144 South Prospect Street, Tucson, Arizona 85705
a.alverez@xxx.com
(520) 555-7348

Office   RTK Consultants
2514 Cleary Road, Tucson, Arizona 85721
(520) 555-7939

EMPLOYMENT HISTORY

2/99 to Present
Wastewater Engineer, RTK Consultants

Design of Wastewater Treatment Facilities

- *Burnett Manufacturing, Inc.:* Managed industrial wastewater treatment plant upgrade, including VOC emissions evaluation of plant using the EPA SIMS and CMA PAVE models. Assessed potential emissions as related to proposed EPA HON regulations. Evaluated biological nitrification of existing plant and proposed upgrade. Developed biological nitrification model to predict plant performance.

- *Revco Industries:* Directed evaluation of toxic air emissions from proposed wastewater treatment plant. Used EPA SIMS and NCASI NOCEPM models. Developed emission reduction plan to demonstrate compliance with state and EPA MACT regulations.

Computer Modeling/Simulation

- Successful development of computer models to optimize wastewater treatment plant's performance for clients in manufacturing, chemical, and food-processing industries.

- Use of KENTUCKY pipe network simulation model to design improvements to existing water and sanitary sewer infrastructures for municipal clients nationwide.

EPA Consultant

- Assisted EPA Office of Solid Waste with environmental regulatory analyses. Used groundwater transport modeling to evaluate proposed land disposal restrictions in hazardous waste legislation. Inspected Class V underground disposal wells as EPA representative. Conducted groundwater sampling at Superfund site.

EMPLOYMENT HISTORY (CONTINUED)

7/96 to 2/99
Product Engineer, Western Telecommunications Inc.

- Developed product specifications and cost containment strategies for manufacture of copper wire and insulation.

- Assisted production management with analysis and innovation of production processes related to solvent reclamation.

- Designed successful automated system for faster material changes.

CREDENTIALS

- B.S., Environmental Engineering, University of Arizona, 1996

- Member, Air and Waste Management Association

- Member, American Society of Technical Engineers

- Languages: Spanish and Italian

References on Request

ADBAR JALIL

661 S. Weston Rd.
Denver, CO 80203
adbar.jalil@xxx.com
303-555-4059

EXPERIENCE

February 2004 to Present
Research Assistant
University of Colorado, Denver, CO

• Leader of Oxidant Research Team charged with analysis of vertical distribution of speciated hydrocarbons and radiosonde measurement of atmospheric conditions.

• Planned and implemented study.

• Direct staff of four research associates.

February 2002 to February 2004
Lecturer, Meteorology
University of Colorado, Denver, CO

• Part-time instructor.

• Taught Fundamentals of Meteorology I and II, undergraduate AB classes.

• Responsible for course preparation, setup and maintenance of lab, student evaluations.

August 2001 to February 2004
Lab Chemist
Hudson Manufacturing Group, Boulder, CO

• Part-time position in chemistry lab, verifying formaldehyde content of particle board and other construction materials for compliance to OSHA standards.

EDUCATION

University of Colorado
Denver, CO

June 2001
Master of Science, Atmospheric Science

June 1999
Bachelor of Science, Environmental Studies
Minor: Chemistry

ACHIEVEMENTS

September 2006
Research grant awarded by National Air Quality Control Council for Vertical
Distribution Study of Carbonyls for Ozone Control.

May 2005
Presentation: Nonmethane Hydrocarbons and Ozone Control.
Annual Conference of Geophysical Research Academy

REFERENCES

References and writing samples available.

Margaret Chapman

9484 N. Ellis St., Baltimore, MD 21203

maggie.chapman@xxx.com

410-555-3949 - Home

410-555-5902 - Cell

Overview

Ten years of experience as an editor and technical writer preparing publications and proposals for the scientific community. Experienced in production of books, academic journals, newsletters, brochures, EPA environmental impact reports, permit applications. Computer literate and capable of overseeing documents through all phases of development from research through publication.

Skills

Technical Writing

- Preparation of EPA toxicology and pesticide reports for Actron Corporation
- Creation of environmental impact statements and sections of EPA reports to Congress for Bartlett Communications Group
- Development of newsletter articles on microelectronics and biomedical engineering for the University of Maryland Publications Division
- Creation of criteria documents at American Environmental Health, Inc., for submission to the National Institute of Occupational Safety and Health

Editing

- Solicit manuscripts, supervise peer review, hire and manage copyeditors and proofreaders, submit camera-ready copy to printer as managing editor for *Journal of Modern Microbiology*
- Copyedit numerous educational publications produced by the University of Maryland

Employment History

University of Maryland Publications Division
Managing Editor, *Journal of Modern Microbiology*, 2005 to Present

University of Maryland Publications Division
Associate Editor of Educational Materials, 2003 to 2005

Actron Corporation
Senior Technical Writer, 2001 to 2003

Bartlett Communications Group
Technical Editor, 2000 to 2001

American Environmental Health, Inc.
Technical Communications Specialist, 1998 to 2000

Education

B.S., University of Maryland, 1998
Double major in English and Microbiology

References and writing samples are available on request.

✦ martin wong

2522 Breckinridge Road
Madison, Wisconsin 53716
m.wong@xxx.com
(608) 555-3445

✦ product engineer

- Computer-aided design (CAD) experience
- Product development and improvement using illustration, model-making, and computer modeling skills
- Marker rendering and mechanical drawing
- Standardization of manufacturing operating procedures
- Technical support for electronics manufacturing divisions
- Lead a team of three

✦ credentials

B.S., University of Wisconsin, Madison, 1998

Engineering Registration #86410

Member, Institute of Industrial Engineers

✦ employment history

Manufacturing Engineer, June 2001 to Present

Lincoln Manufacturing, Madison, Wisconsin

Product Designer, June 1998 to June 2001

Haverford Electronics, Chicago, Illinois

✦ references

Personal and professional references on request

Examples of work available for review at www.martin-wong.com

MICHELLE COOK

640 S. Long St.
Boston, MA 02116
(617) 555-5306 - Home
(617) 555-1202 - Cellular
m.cook@xxx.com

EXPERTISE

EDITORIAL: Experienced content editor and copyeditor with specialization in scientific topics. Competent desktop publisher, experienced in Quark Express and InDesign. Accurate proofreader.

TEACHING: Certified secondary education teacher with experience teaching biology and chemistry.

RESEARCH: Competent research assistant with strong lab skills and experience in statistical analysis.

EMPLOYERS

Journal of American Science
Assistant Editor, 2002 to 2005

St. Steven's Academy
Science Teacher, 2001 to 2002

University of Maryland, Department of Biology
Laboratory Assistant, 2000

EDUCATION

B.S., University of Maryland, 2001
MAJOR: Education
MINOR: Biology

References on request.

WALTER SMITH

8766 Sycamore Trail
Des Plaines, IL 60018
(847) 555-7784 Work
(847) 555-9705 Home

OBJECTIVE

Computer Programming and Systems Analysis

Technical Expertise Databases: DB2, RAMIS

Languages: Programatically-generated HTML, DHTML, Client side JavaScript, Server side VBScript TELON

Hardware: IBM mainframe and PCs

PC Software: WordPerfect, Excel, Access, Lotus 1-2-3

Other Tools: Background in C#, technical writing, Linux

OVERVIEW

▌ Systems experience in an MVSXA operating system 30XX class IBM machines and IBM PC/LAN workstations

▌ Experience at the division level, including the automation of sales tracking, budget/forecast models, and user training

▌ Proven record of delivering computerized systems under tight deadlines to meet exacting requirements

▌ Training and supervisory experience

Page 1 of 2

PROFESSIONAL EXPERIENCE

***Programmer Analyst II, Hansbury Manufacturing, Inc.,
2000 to Present***
Develop software programs and routines for commercial computer-based
software, interactive courseware, desktop publishing, multimedia,
client/server, n-tier, and Internet technologies for training applications.
Analyze, update, repair, and modify software code and documented
routines of existing software programs. Test hardware and evaluate and
correct software deficiencies, including packaged software and
courseware, to insure instructions will produce the desired results.

***Senior Programmer Analyst, Harrison Research Group,
1995 to 2000***
Led a seven-member team installing TransEXPRESS distribution system
that reduced freight-printed output by 9.4 percent. Created workplans,
headcount utilization, program specifications, and user training.
Converted all CICS programs to new system, updating JCL and
complying to new system standards. Provided application support of the
freight/DCMS system.

References Available

JAY ALLEN

611 Trenton Road ✦ Sacramento, CA 95819
jay.allen@xxx.com ✦ (916) 555-9861

BACKGROUND

- Certified Professional Erosion and Sediment Control Specialist
- Seven years with California Soil Conservation Service
- Three years with Department of Agriculture's Natural Resource Conservation Service
- Knowledge of statistics and Global Positioning Systems (GPS) survey techniques

WORK HISTORY

Soil Conservationist, 2000 to Present
State of California, Soil Conservation Service

- Visit outdoor recreation, wildlife, and agricultural sites to assess erosion problems.
- Develop and implement land management programs to maintain soil stability and vegetation.
- Plan and implement revegetation of disturbed sites.
- Compile statistics and submit written analyses to agency director for legislative use.

Conservation Technician, 1997 to 2000
Department of Agriculture, Natural Resource Conservation Service

- Participated in quality control management for flood control and dam projects undertaken in conjunction with the U.S. Army Corps of Engineers.
- Monitored contracting and construction personnel on-site to ensure proper excavation techniques and compliance with federal guidelines.

CREDENTIALS

B.A. in Environmental Studies, 1997
University of California at San Diego
Minor: Statistics

- Member, Soil and Water Conservation Society
- Certification in Soil Erosion and Sediment Control awarded by the Soil and Water Conservation Society, 2004
- Courses in GPS techniques sponsored by American Society for Photogrammetry and Remote Sensing

REFERENCES

References and writing samples are available on request.

KEVIN WEST

• • • • • • • • • • • • • • • • • •

9325 South Oak Street
Dallas, Texas 75243
kevin.west@xxx.com
(214) 555-9406

Goal

Opportunity to fully utilize industrial engineering and process engineering skills while working for a midsize manufacturing firm

Skills

- Cost reduction
- Thorough knowledge of methods standards
- Expert in manufacturing layout designs
- Problem solving of floor production problems
- Knowledge of metal fabrication/assembly
- Equipment justification and line-balancing skills

Employment

Senior Industrial Engineer, Alcor Engineering, Inc.
January 2002 to Present

Industrial Design Engineer, CBI Manufacturing
May 1996 to January 2002

Credentials

B.S., Industrial Engineering, Purdue University, 1996
Registered Engineer

Affiliations

Member, Institute of Industrial Engineers

References on request

Carmen Delgato

197 Compton Street

Chicago, IL 60618

carmen.delgato@xxx.com

(312) 555-6978

Work History

10/02 to Present
Director of Education and Community Relations • Midwest Science Center

- Develop and implement all staff training and in-service programming

- Supervise publication of in-house newsletter, press releases, and educational literature

- Design and direct marketing/community relations campaigns and special events

- Media contact/museum spokesperson

8/96 to 10/02
Marketing Manager • Baker & West Healthcare Systems

- Directed marketing efforts for multinational medical equipment firm

- Managed staff of 14 marketing professionals

- Developed marketing surveys and compiled statistics

- Issued press releases

- Designed multimedia campaigns in support of new products

6/92 to 8/96
Technical Writer • Baker & West Healthcare Systems

- Developed equipment product literature, including pharmaceutical inserts, technical manuals, and brochures

- Wrote and edited marketing literature and other projects when needed

Page 1 of 2

Education

B.A., University of Delaware, 1992
Technical Communications Major

Credentials

Member, American Marketing Association
Member, Society of Technical Writers

References on request

LAWRENCE T. DAVIS

573 Perry Road
East Hampton, NY 11937
E-mail: l.davis@xxx.com
Cell: 631-555-7382

Goal

Full-time position teaching Biology and/or other Life Sciences at the secondary level.

Experience

Science Instructor, East Hampton Academy, 6/04 to Present

- Responsible for college prep science curriculum at private school with 200 students.
- Courses include Biology, Physics, and Chemistry.
- Organize all aspects of the annual science fair.
- Set up and maintain chemistry lab.
- Supervise peer-tutoring program.

Laboratory Assistant, Mendecott Laboratories, 8/00 to 6/04

- Assisted chemical researchers with laboratory experiments and statistical analysis of data.
- Compiled statistics and maintained database.
- Prepared written and oral status reports.

Credentials

B.S., University of Maryland, 2000
Double Major in Life Sciences and Education

A.S., New England Community College, 1998
Major in Biology

Member, National Education Association

Secondary teaching certifications in New York and Maryland

References available upon request.

LISA HOLMES

4226 Pleasant Road
Milwaukee, WI 53205
414-555-7986 (work)
414-555-8997 (cell)

OBJECTIVE:

Opportunity for continued professional development and community service providing educational development services to a midsize nonprofit group.

EXPERIENCE:

Midwest Botanical Gardens
Director of Educational Development Programs
September 2002 to Present

- Design and implement educational programs in the following areas: staff development, public school educational tours, garden club tours, and community outreach.
- Implemented fund-raising and grant-writing projects that increased department's budget by 15 percent.
- Increased benefactor's donations to the Memorial Garden by 10 percent last year.

Walker Science Museum
Manager, Children's Discovery Center
January 1999 to September 2002

- Supervised and enhanced visitor use of enclosed children's center within museum.
- Designed and supervised special events.
- Provided yearly expenses and budgets.

EDUCATION:

B.S., University of Wisconsin, 2002
Major: Education
Minor: Botany

REFERENCES:

Available on request.

RACHEL DYKSTRA

▮ 2513 Alcott Street, #106
▮ Chicago, IL 60645
▮ (312) 555-8611 Home
▮ (312) 555-4978 Work
▮ rdykstra@xxx.com

▮ PROFESSIONAL SKILLS

Managerial

▮ Industrial production management experience, including daily supervision and coordination of all production activities for firm producing fabricated metal products

▮ Coordination of interdepartmental production schedules

▮ Responsible for training, supervision, and staffing duties

▮ Development and enforcement of safety standards

Financial

▮ Cost estimating

▮ Cost accounting

▮ Purchasing

▮ Inventory control

Technical

▮ CAD/CAM drafting and design skills

▮ Knowledge of machining, assembly, and finishing

▮ EMPLOYMENT HISTORY

National Metals, Production Manager, 2000 to Present
Warner Electronics, Floor Supervisor, 1997 to 2000
David Wright & Associates, Machinist, 1990 to 1997

▮ EDUCATION

M.B.A.   Northwestern University, Evanston, IL   2000
B.S.   Northern Illinois University, DeKalb, IL   1990
            Major: Business

▮ MEMBERSHIPS

▮ American Production and Inventory Control Society

▮ National Management Association

▮ COMMUNITY SERVICE

▮ Volunteer carpenter, Habitat for Humanity

▮ Board member, Mayor's Council on Recycling & Environmental Awareness

▮ REFERENCES AVAILABLE

Latisha Brown, MSN

9877 S. Rodgers Court
Trammel, TX 55432
lbrown@xxx.com
(303) 555-7163

Experience

Project Manager, 9/05 to Present
Comprehensive Immunization Initiative, Texas Nursing Foundation

- Working to develop educational programs for health-care professionals, design public health programs, and establish goals for improved immunization service and delivery to all children by age 24 months.

Educational Specialist, 2/03 to 9/05
Helen White Nursing Scholar Program, National Nursing Academy

- Assisted Director of Endowments in reviewing scholarly abstracts to select recipients of grants in public health nursing.

Board Member, 1/96 to 2/03
Texas Board of Nursing

- Appointed to serve state nursing board as consultant on professional issues, including nursing licensure, disciplinary measures, school accreditation, and establishment of nursing practices and procedures.

Education

MSN, University of Texas, 1996

References Available

Ted MacFarland

2336 Milwaukee Road

Columbus, Ohio 43266

Ted.MacFarland@xxx.com

(614) 555-8316

Objective

Applied research position that will utilize my academic background in astronomy and skills as an educator and researcher.

Previous Employment

September 2000 to Present
Program Director, Covington Planetarium

≡ Manage the "Night Skies" program of planetarium shows for students and the general public.
≡ Oversee staffing, maintenance of all equipment, and preparation of supplemental educational materials.
≡ Coordinate with the marketing director to promote the program.

April 1996 to August 2000
Research Associate, University of Washington

≡ Assisted chair of physics/astronomy department with research in crystallography.
≡ Duties included database management, observation, computer modeling, and creation of status reports.

Credentials

University of Michigan, B.S., 1996
Major: Astronomy; Minor: Physics

Member, American Astronomical Society

References

A list of references will be provided on request.

ALICE BROOKS

89 East Truman Avenue
East Hampton, NY 11937
(631) 555-6902 Work
(631) 555-4958 Home
Alice.Brooks@xxx.com

Experience

- Background in surveying and cartography.
- Experience with federal agencies and with private architectural and engineering firms.
- Comfortable with both Global Positioning System (GPS) and Geographic Information Systems (GIS) technology.
- Computer-aided design (CAD) and drafting experience.
- Experienced in legal land title and boundary searches.

Recent Employment

Director of Building Permits Division, October 2000 to Present
East Hampton Department of Public Works, East Hampton, NY

- Review title and permit requests.
- Subcontract building inspection and land survey services.
- Ensure compliance with state and county building and fire safety codes.
- Contribute to long-range planning efforts of land management and public safety committees of county government.
- Manage a staff of five employees.

Recent Employment (continued)

Land Surveyor, March 1998 to October 2000
Klein Design Inc., Guilford, CT (subsidiary of Miles & Brimelow Properties)

- Directed land survey parties in fieldwork to establish precise boundaries and significant topographical features of proposed building sites.
- Researched prior boundaries as necessary to establish legal lot lines.
- Prepared maps, plats, and reports.

Credentials

- B.S., Surveying, Syracuse University, 1998
- Licensed Surveyor, State of Connecticut R3609
- International Conference of Building Inspectors (ICBO)
- Certified Plans Examiner and Building Inspector
- Member, American Congress on Surveying and Mapping

References and portfolio furnished on request.

Maria Sabatini

978 Old Mill Road • Philadelphia, PA 20036 • m.sabatini@xxx.com • 215-555-4655

Objective

Position as a Restoration Architect.

Summary

- Proven management and client-relations ability.
- Train and motivate staff.
- Superior written and verbal communications skills, create successful client presentations.
- Project management experience.
- Able to manage several concurrent projects and conclude each on time and within budget.

Job History

Restoration Architect, Winston and Bell, Philadelphia, PA • 2002 to present

- Restoration of historic commercial and industrial buildings, private residences, and governmental structures.
- Responsible for determining clients' goals, analyzing existing condition of structure, researching historical development of building, producing preliminary sketches for clients' approval, developing project outline and cost estimates, preparing construction documents and drawings, selecting contractor, and visiting construction site to monitor progress.

Design Architect, Crosscurrents Design, Philadelphia, PA • 1999 to 2002

- Responsible for drafting, blueprint development, space planning, and design for ecological planning firm.
- Interfaced with architects and subcontractors.

Drafter, TLJ Construction, Watertown, MA • 1996 to 1999

- Responsible for creation of blueprints and scale models, surveying work, and on-site inspections.

Education and License

B.A in Architecture, University of Pennsylvania, 1996
Pennsylvania #R-6211

REFERENCES PROVIDED ON REQUEST

SONJA WINCHESTER, D.V.M.

232 Pearl Street
Ypsilanti, MI 48197
s.winchester@xxx.com
(734) 555-2716

OBJECTIVE

Full-time veterinarian position in animal hospital or clinic with opportunity for eventual supervisory responsibilities.

EXPERIENCE

Extensive experience in small-animal practice providing both routine and emergency care. Excellent diagnostic and surgical skills. Strong interpersonal and communications skills.

EMPLOYERS

Easthaven Animal Clinic
Ann Arbor, MI
June 2004 to Present

Brighton Veterinary Hospital
Brighton, MI
April 2001 to June 2004

CREDENTIALS

D.V.M.
Michigan State University, 2001

Licensed D.V.M., Michigan

Member, American Veterinary Medical Association

References available upon request.

JESSICA BAHIRINI

3630 South Fenton Road
Cleveland, Ohio 44106
(216) 555-1197 Work
(216) 555-8091 Home
jbahirini@xxx.com

BACKGROUND

Talented clinical dietician with experience in long-term care
and home health agency settings. Seeking full-time position
with supervisory responsibilities.

WORK HISTORY

HTL Home Health Ltd.
Supervisor, Nutritional Assistance Program
2004 to Present

- Supervise staff of four dieticians working to provide
  community dietician services via home health agency.

- Oversee the development of nutritional care plans.

- Train, supervise, and support dieticians in assessing
  clients' health status and nutritional needs.

- Assist dieticians in training clients and family members in
  proper nutrition and food preparation.

William and Mary Medical Center Level II
Clinical Dietician
2001 to 2004

- Provided nutritional services for nursing home patients.

- Assessed patients' nutritional needs, developed and
  implemented nutritional programs with assistance from
  medical staff.

- Evaluated and reported on patient progress.

- Coordinated medical and nutritional therapies.

CREDENTIALS

B.S., Case Western Reserve, 1997
Major: Dietetics

Registered Dietician
Member of American Dietetic Association
CPR Certified

PUBLICATIONS

"The Value of Vegetarian Diets for AIDS Patients: Assessing the Options," *American Journal of Psychology*, July 2006.

"The Fine Print: Labeling and Fat-Free Products," *Home Health News*, May 2005.

REFERENCES

Available on request.

❖ Karen S. Martin ❖

518 N. Kingston Ct., #215
Lafayette, IN 47905
k.martin@xxx.com
214-555-6968

❖ Objective ❖

Full-time entry-level environmental engineering position.

❖ Education ❖

M.S., Environmental Engineering
Purdue University, 2004

B.S., Civil Engineering
Purdue University, 2002

Courses:

◆ Air Pollution Control and Design

◆ Air Quality

◆ Management Facilities Design

◆ Geotechnical Engineering

◆ Transportation Design

❖ Work History ❖

Environmental Engineering Specialist
Trenton Engineering, 7/04 to Present
Duties: Acquisition and analysis of environmental data.

Civil Engineer, part-time
Barton Construction, 8/02 to 7/04
Duties: Quality control inspection for transportation projects. Ensure compliance with state standards for asphalt density using nuclear density meter.

References available upon request.

Alicia Perez

23 Vero Beach Blvd. • Maitland, FL 55632
607-555-8987 (Cell) • Alicia.Perez@xxx.com

Goal

Seeking information management position with public or school library.

Skills

Managerial Ability: On-site supervision of librarians and library volunteers. Coordination and scheduling of all work done by library staff.

Computer Skills: Knowledge of FORTRAN, Pascal, and Basic programming languages; Windows and Macintosh systems; and Word and Excel software.

Technical Knowledge: Extensive knowledge of environmental and organic chemistry and related public policy.

Library Science Skills: Design and management of information retrieval systems. Maintain, develop, and index databases. Index, abstracting, and research skills with scientific and technical applications.

Employers

Richardson Center for Scientific Research
Head Librarian, 2004 to Present

Maitland Public Library System
Automation Specialist, 2000 to 2004

Education

M.L.S., University of Florida, Gainesville, 2000

M.S., University of Florida, Gainesville, 1998
Major: Chemistry

B.S., Florida Technical College, Auburndale, 1996
Major: Computer Science; Minor: Chemistry

Affiliations

Member, American Society for Information Science
Member, Special Libraries Association

References

List of references and writing samples are available.

Kenneth Orrico

808 S. Fairmont Rd.

Arlington, VA 22202

Ken.Orrico@xxx.com

703-555-6375 Work

703-555-3061 Home

Objective	Environmental educator position with small museum or nonprofit organization
Education	M.S. in Environmental Studies University of Maryland, 2004 B.A. in Education New England Teachers College, 2000
Certification	Secondary Teaching Certification State of Maryland, 2000
Experience	Activity Director, 6/04 to Present Burlington Center for Environmental Studies Curriculum Consultant, 6/02 to 6/04 Virginia Academy of Sciences Laboratory Assistant, 10/00 to 6/02 University of Maryland
Affiliations	New England Association for Environmental Education National Education Association
References	References and writing samples on request

Elizabeth Morgan

220 Randall Road
Corvallis, OR 97331
Liz.Morgan@xxx.com
541-555-4059 Work
541-555-6907 Home

Work Experience

2001 to Present
Research Technician, Oregon Institute for Meteorological Research

- Develop and modify FORTRAN programs to process and analyze atmospheric data
- Adapt MATLAB programs to provide further data analysis and computer graphics
- Launch and track radiosondes
- Calibrate equipment and monitor tracking devices
- Collect atmospheric data on aerosols
- Track pilot balloons using a theodolite

Education

B.S., Meteorology
Oregon State University, 2001

Skills

Proficient in MATLAB, FORTRAN, Microsoft Word, VMS, and Turbo C++

References available

ELLEN PI HONG

6212 North Washington Street
Cleveland, Ohio 44115
(216) 555-1905 Work
(216) 555-8277 Home
Ellen.Hong@xxx.com

GOAL:

Air quality specialist position that utilizes my knowledge of monitoring, modeling, and health-risk assessment.

EXPERIENCE:

Midwest Environmental Testing Consultants
Air Quality Specialist, 2002 to Present

- Oversee industrial hygiene and air-monitoring projects.

- Operate ambient monitoring programs serving public utilities clients.

- Install, operate, maintain, calibrate, and repair computerized ambient air and meteorological monitoring equipment.

- Prepare daily and weekly reports.

- Compile quarterly monitoring data for submission to regulatory agencies.

- Write and update data acquisitions software in C and Basic.

- Oversee asbestos abatement projects, including air monitoring, on-site analysis, and disposal of asbestos waste.

CREDENTIALS:

B.S. in Atmospheric Science
Northern Illinois University, 2002

Certified Public Health Inspector
State of Ohio, Department of Public Safety

MEMBERSHIPS:

Air and Waste Management Association
Midwest Council for Air Quality Control

REFERENCES:

Available on request.

Paul Grant ❖ Certified Physician Assistant

522 Ivy Lane
Brookings, SD 57007
paulgrant@xxx.com
(605) 555-3889

Employment History

2004 to Present
Director, Corneal Transplant Program
South Dakota State University Eye Clinic

- ❖ Manage all aspects of the corneal transplant program.

- ❖ Duties include tracing donors through nationwide computer database, supervising tissue typing, arranging the harvesting and transport of donor organs, counseling donor families, and obtaining formal consents.

- ❖ Direct clerical staff of two.

- ❖ Design and implement community outreach plan to increase awareness of need for donor organs.

2000 to 2004
Ophthalmology Assistant, Department of Ophthalmology
St. Patrick's Hospital

- ❖ Provided full range of physician assistant services in hospital ophthalmology department with annual census of 25,000 patients.

- ❖ Facilitated SDSU organ donations when possible, counseling patient families and securing initial consents.

- ❖ Developed in-service program to educate staff on obtaining organ donation consents.

Education

B.S.   South Dakota State University
1997   Physician Assistant Program

Certifications

PA-C   Certified Physician Assistant
CPR   Red Cross CPR Certification

References

Both personal and professional references are available upon request.

MICHAEL AHMED

3647 South Hancock Street

Santa Fe, New Mexico 87501

(505) 555-1776 Cell

(505) 555-0798 Home

Mike.Ahmed@xxx.com

GOAL

Opportunity to produce polished technical communications on environmental topics.

EXPERIENCE

Edited and produced procedure and training manuals for hazardous waste disposal. Created employee training manual for educational consulting firm specializing in asbestos abatement programs. Developed text and maps for visitor guides for National Parks Service.

EDUCATION

M.A., University of New Mexico, 2004
American Studies with an Ecology concentration

B.A., University of New Mexico, 2002
Technical Communications concentration

WORK HISTORY

2002 to 2004
J.S. Spencer Environmental Services
Environmental Communications Consultant, part-time

2000 to 2002
National Parks Service
Student Intern

References Available

DAN WILLIAMSON

749 S. Culverton Rd.
Davis, CA 95616
d.williamson@xxx.com
916-555-7258

Background

❖ Air quality technician with extensive experience in quality assurance testing

❖ Install and monitor sampling equipment at field sites

❖ Compile and analyze data

❖ Generate reports from collected data

Employment

Lakehurst Air Quality Specialists
Researcher, January 2001 to Present

Essex Environmental Group
Field Technician, September 1998 to January 2001

National Parks Service
Research Assistant, January 1997 to September 1998

Education

M.S. in Ecology
University of California, Davis, 1997

B.S. in Chemistry
Kenyon College, 1995

References Available

✳ *Keiko Kobayashi* ✳

844 S. Essex Rd.
East Greenwich, RI 02818
K.Kobayashi@xxx.com
401-555-7319

Goal	Software Engineering Position
Credentials	M.I.S., Rhode Island Technical Institute B.S., Queens College
	VAX and Micro VAX, Intel Software, C++, Unix Systems, MS Windows, VMS, Pascal, BASIC, PHP, SYQL
Experience	*Princeton Computer Supplies, 9/04 to Present* Senior Systems Designer
	Develop I/O interfaces and create/support file transfer systems. Extensive use of Intel software and VAX in C++ Language.
	Superior Software, 6/01 to 9/04 Technical Advisor
	Marketing and sales support for software products, including spreadsheets, word processing programs, graphics, and database applications.
	Little & Young Development, 5/98 to 6/01 Team leader for software development projects.
	Promoted after one year from programmer to senior programmer.
References	Available on request.

James Weldon

483 S. Rice St.
Cleveland, OH 44138
James.Weldon@xxx.com
(216) 555-5145

Background

Technical supervisor with specialization in data processing, familiar with UNISYS equipment and CICS systems programming.

Expertise

DOS/VSE	IMS	EASYTRIEVE
CICS	NCP	COBOL
DL1	VTAM	C++
Windows	BASIC	PHP

Employment

Bradley Manufacturing
Data Processing Supervisor, 7/92 to Present

Direct start-up of new data control center, including installation of all workstations and peripheral equipment. Establish data control procedures. Assist in hiring and training new staff.

Star Data Corporation
Database Manager, 4/91 to 7/92

Managed data processing department, including all data entry and output, using UNISYS equipment. Supervised staff of eight.

Employment *continued*

APT Chemical Corporation
Data Control Specialist, 6/86 to 4/91

Responsible for maintenance of 150-terminal network. Supported online batch order processing function.

Education

B.S., Information Technology
Ohio State University, 1986

References available.

Sarah K. Bednar

911 West Street
Ann Arbor, MI 48766
sarah.bednar@xxx.com
(734) 555-9874

BACKGROUND

Computer programmer/analyst with extensive experience installing, testing, and maintaining financial systems

TECHNICAL SKILLS

COBOL	DB2	MS/OS
EASYTRIEVE	IDMS	MS Windows
BASIC	RAMIS	TSO/ISPF
Pascal	Oracle (PC)	CICS
C++	SYQL Server	Telon
Panvalet	Roscoe	PHP

APPLICATIONS

- Installation and maintenance of financial systems for general ledger, check reconciliation, inventory, and cash management systems

- Creation of program specifications

- Installation of bug-fix tapes and hand fixes

- Maintenance and development of mainframe systems

EMPLOYERS

Quinn Automotive, Ann Arbor
9/02 to Present, Programmer/Analyst

Small Business Council, Ann Arbor
9/01 to 9/02, Consultant

Best Foods, Detroit
6/99 to 9/01, Systems Analyst

LT Chemical, Detroit
6/96 to 6/99, Systems Analyst

EDUCATION

M.I.S.
Stanford University, 1996

B.S., Information Technology
University of Michigan, 1994

REFERENCES

Available

DRAYTON T. JACKSON

3316 Western Road

Lake Forest, CA 92630

D.Jackson@xxx.com

(714) 555-6150

OVERVIEW

▐ Experienced EMT capable of responding to wide variety of trauma cases at the scene.

▐ Currently seeking RN licensure.

▐ Strong commitment to career in trauma services.

EDUCATION

A.S., Emergency Medical Technology
Lake Forest Community College, 2003

B.S.N., Nursing
University of California, degree expected 2007

Board-certified EMT

CPR Instructor

EXPERIENCE

Lake Forest Community Rescue Team, 2005 to Present

▐ Team leader for urban mobile trauma unit.

▐ Interface with hospital ER staff by phone to provide trauma management en route from accident scenes.

▐ Stabilize patients for transport.

▐ Train and monitor dispatchers.

Page 1 of 2

EXPERIENCE
CONTINUED

Warren County Fire and Rescue Service, 2003 to 2005

▌ EMT duties.

▌ CPR instructor for firefighters and EMTs.

▌ Provided CPR certification programs for community groups as requested.

REFERENCES AVAILABLE

DOUG NELSON

2811 Clark Street
Boulder, CO 80302
Doug.Nelson@xxx.com
(303) 555-9386

Overview

Professional technical editor and writer specializing in medical and scientific subjects. Experienced magazine editor. Competent production of technical documents, brochures, newsletters, and scientific documentation.

Skills

- Proofreading. • Content editing. • Copyediting.
- Technical writing. • Document preparation.

Work History

Associate Editor, American Society of Microbiology
2/03 to Present

Duties: Content editing and copyediting of articles for Journal of Microbiology. Arrange for peer review of articles. Work with authors to resolve queries and polish prose. Review unsolicited manuscripts.

Technical Editor, Claremont Environmental Consultants
6/01 to 2/03

Duties: Production of lengthy environmental status reports. Responsible for editing, rewriting, and proofreading all materials. Responsible for all general production duties.

Work History (continued)

Technical Writer, University of Colorado Publications Department
6/99 to 6/01

Duties: Wrote brochure copy and newsletter articles reporting on ongoing scientific research at the university. Topics included Microbiology, Physics, and Engineering.

Credentials

B.S., Ohio State University, 1999
Major: Biology
Minor: English

Member, American Society of Technical Communicators

Personal and professional references available.
Writing samples submitted on request.

Henry Yee

8722 Lucas Street

Des Moines, Iowa 50309

H.Yee@xxx.com

(515) 555-6207

SUMMARY

Experienced freelance technical writer seeking clients.

SKILLS

- Developing product proposals
- Content editing and copyediting technical documents
- Revising/updating technical manuals
- Conducting research projects
- Preparing documentation for software products
- Creating revision reports for technical engineers

CLIENTS

- Jenkins Engineering
- Cooper Technical Publications
- Electronic Design Inc.
- Jones & Little Environmental Consultants
- York Communications

CREDENTIALS

B.S., University of Wisconsin, 2003
Computer Science

Member, Society for Technical Communications

REFERENCES

Available on request

MARIA CRUZE

643 Gleason Street • St. Michaels, MD 21652

Cellular: 410-555-3409 • E-mail: maria.cruze@xxx.net

CREDENTIALS

B. Arch., University of Maryland, 2002

- GPA of 3.5.
- Earned 75 percent of expenses through part-time employment in building trades.
- Winner of McIntyre Architectural Scholarship and Senior Design Award.

License: #R-6877, issued by State of Maryland, 2003

SKILLS

- CAD/CAM design experience.
- Specifications writing.
- On-site project management.
- Fluent in Spanish.

EMPLOYERS

Robinson Design Group, St. Michaels, MD
Architectural Draftsman, May 2004 to Present

Carlson Associates, Baltimore, MD
Design Assistant, June 2002 to April 2004

R.T.W. Construction, Baltimore, MD
Construction Worker, Summers 1999 to 2001

REFERENCES

Available upon request.

T E R R A N C E K I N G

765 Crestview Road   *Monterey, CA 90766*
Terrance.King@xxx.com   *202-555-9686*

GOAL

Professional experience in design, architecture, and historical preservation

ASSETS

- Extensive knowledge of interior design, architecture, and preservation
- Excellent supervisor, manage a staff of eight
- Highly organized and meticulous
- Effective fund-raiser for projects
- Skilled communicator with a strong background in presentation

AREAS OF EXPERTISE

Design

- Created interior designs for 20 model homes in five locations statewide for a major residential builder.
- Responsible for color schemes, space planning, furniture selection, and window treatments.
- Completed all designs to supervisor's satisfaction.
- All work completed on time and within budget.

BUSINESS MANAGEMENT

- Recruited and trained 12 volunteers for San Francisco Preservation Council.
- Developed standard office procedures for Robinson & Associates, an architectural firm.
- Generated and maintained all project documents, contracts, and client files.
- Developed and executed direct-mail campaign that raised $40,000 for San Francisco Preservation Council.

Page 1 of 2

PROFESSIONAL HISTORY

Director, San Francisco Preservation Council
June 2004 to Present

Designer, Lexington Builders
May 2000 to June 2004

Office Manager, Robinson & Associates
January 1996 to April 2000

EDUCATION

San Francisco City College
B.S. in Accounting, 2004

University of California, Los Angeles
B.A. in Interior Design, 1999

REFERENCES AVAILABLE

SUSAN E. WILDER

962 Redmond Road
Melbourne, FL 32902
407-555-0179
susan.wilder@xxx.com

BACKGROUND

Nurse educator seeking tenure-track assistant or associate professor position at nationally recognized research university.

RECENT EXPERIENCE

Florida State University, Center for Nursing Practice
Assistant Professor of Nursing, 1998–Present
Responsible for maternal-child courses for RN-BSN program.

Melbourne Memorial Hospital
Education Specialist, 1995–1998
Designed and implemented nursing orientation program. Monitored nursing preceptor program. Designed and implemented community health education programs.

St. Francis Care Center
Director of Nursing, 1991–1995
Managed nursing staff for 50-bed substance abuse recovery program.

RESEARCH

Currently completing ongoing prevention and behavioral research at Florida State University regarding HIV-positive newborns.

Recently awarded ANA grant to pursue research on clinical issues and trends in early intervention for developmentally delayed infants.

PUBLICATIONS

"Beating the Odds: Prenatal Care and Teenage Mothers," *American Nurse,* October 1999.

"Discharge Planning for the Addicted Newborn: Assuring Quality Care in the Home," *Social Services Weekly,* June 2000.

EDUCATION

MSN   University of Missouri, 1991
BSN   Marycrest College, 1989

CERTIFICATIONS

PALS
CPR
ACLS
TNS

REFERENCES

Available

Tom Nguent

789 North Grant Street
Tulsa, OK 74101
T.Nguent@xxx.com
(918) 555-9868

Professional Experience

Urban Planning
Consult with city and county governments on community development. Inspect sites for new and expanding communities. Ensure compliance with municipal building codes once projects are underway.

Environmental Testing
Collected and analyzed samples to assess air quality, water pollution. Inspected suspected sites of pollution and issued status reports and recommendations for intervention.

Land Management
Responsible for stream and timber management. Conducted educational tours of wetlands. Created topographical maps.

Employment

City of Tulsa, Department of Community Development
Job Title: Urban Planning Consultant
Dates: May 2000 to Present

Oklahoma Environmental Agency
Job Title: Public Health Inspector
Dates: May 1996 to April 2000

Washington State Bureau of Land Management
Job Title: Environmental Engineer
Dates: January 1992 to May 1996

Education

B.S., University of Colorado, 1991
Major: Environmental Studies
Minor: Chemistry

References Available on Request

Allison Lightfeather ❧ *Landscape Architect*

809 S. Park St.
Boulder, CO 80304
alightfeather@xxx.com
303-555-6948

Experience ❧

Powell Design Inc.   *1999 to Present*

Owner of landscape design firm specializing in commercial and multiunit residential projects. Work in cooperation with architects and interior designers.

Colorado Community College   *1999 to Present*

Lecturer on Landscape Design. Teach Horticulture 101 and Basic Landscaping.

Grady Nursery   *1997 to 1999*

Assistant manager of nursery. Supervised salespeople, maintained inventory, scheduled deliveries and landscaping projects.

Awards ❧

Businesswoman of the Year
Denver Businesswomen   *2000*

Best Landscape Design
Colorado Design Council   *1999*

Education ❧

University of California at Berkeley
B.S., Landscape Architecture   *1998*

References Available

Andrew Long

9088 S. Warren Rd.

Knoxville, TN 37950

Andy.Long@xxx.com

615-555-5466

Goal

To acquire diversified experience in landscape design.

Recent Projects

Landscape designer for Knoxville Inn, Knoxville
Design and execution of grounds for 30-room inn. Project included design of perennial garden, formal rose garden, fish pond, and fountain. Provided client with preliminary sketches, scale models, detailed budget. Coordinated work of subcontractors.

Gardening Consultant to Green Garden, Inc., Savannah
Consultant to national chain of home-improvement stores. Helped marketing and purchasing executives develop and promote their own line of lawn and garden care products.

Landscape Designer for Arbor Street Cafe, Knoxville
Redesign of front entryway and outdoor eating area in collaboration with interior designer. Planned space, designed garden, and trained client in maintenance techniques.

Employment History

1998 to Present
Self-employed landscape architect

1996 to 1998
Landscape designer, Sterling Garden Services, Knoxville

1992 to 1996
Manager, Savannah Nursery, Savannah

Credentials

Degree
University of Georgia, B.A., 1991
Environmental Design

Memberships
American Institute of Landscape Design
Southern Design Council

Awards
Best Formal Garden, Southern Design Council Contest
Special Achievement Award, Knoxville City Council

References

Available on request

MARY CHANG

654 South Church Street
Grand Rapids, MI 49501
E-mail: Mary.Chang@xxx.com
Home: 616-555-2047
Cell: 616-555-6646

OBJECTIVE

Seeking full-time position in food-processing technology.

EXPERIENCE

Morton Test Kitchens, Nutritional Analyst
623 Dayton Street, Kentwood, MI 49512
1998 to Present

Work with product development staff and test kitchen personnel to verify nutritional content of new products. Analyze levels of additives, vitamins, fats, sugars, and proteins. Record data for input into various databases. Work with product development staff in designing new products that meet federal standards, consumer safety guidelines, and consumer nutritional objectives.

State of Michigan, Department of Public Safety,
*** Sanitation Inspector II***
5991 South Wexler Road, Caledonia, MI 49316
1995 to 1998

Enforced state health codes in industrial settings at food-processing plants and at restaurants applying for operating licensure. Examined all food-processing areas to ensure that sanitation, safety, quality, and waste management standards were met. Developed quality control plans and scheduled follow-up inspections.

Page 1 of 2

EDUCATION

B.S., Georgia State University, 1994
Major: Nutrition

CERTIFICATION

Certified Public Health Inspector, State of Michigan

MEMBERSHIP

Institute for Food Technologists

References are available.

MICHAEL O'BRIEN

261 Arthur Lane
Cleveland, Ohio 44115
Mike.Obrien@xxx.com
(216) 555-4958

BACKGROUND   Licensed electrician with 15 years' experience as contractor/subcontractor for wide variety of commercial, residential, and industrial projects

CREDENTIALS   Ohio License C-4623 7

Certified by Cleveland Technical College Apprenticeship Program

SKILLS   Manage crews of 2 to 12 workers

Train apprentice and journeyman electricians

Ensure on-site safety and quality control

Purchase materials and equipment

Estimate costs

Coordinate with architects, building inspectors, contractors, and subcontractors

Complete wiring for projects, including hospital, nuclear power plant, shopping mall, and apartment complex

EMPLOYMENT   The DiAngelo Company, Master Electrician
1995 to Present

Citizens Electric, General Foreman
1991 to 1995

Cleveland Light, Journeyman Electrician
1989 to 1991

REFERENCES   Available upon request

Sunil Soman

9087 Terrace Street
Newport News, Virginia 23606
Sunil.Soman@xxx.com
804-555-5958

BACKGROUND

State certified speech pathologist and audiologist with master's degree and strong commitment to bringing direct clinical services to individuals with communications disorders. Desire full-time employment in hospital or university setting with potential for advancement to an administrative level.

CREDENTIALS

M.S. from University of Virginia, 1990; graduated with honors; financed 80 percent of tuition by working full-time while carrying full course load.

Certifications:
Certificate of Clinical Competence
American Speech-Language-Hearing Association
Certified for work in Virginia Public Schools

Memberships:
American Academy of Audiology
American Speech-Language-Hearing Association

EMPLOYERS

St. Catherine's Hospital, Speech Pathologist, 1996 to Present
Richmond Clinic, Speech Pathologist, 1990 to 1996

References available upon request.

ANNE LOWENSTEIN

5201 South Selden Street • Tucson, Arizona 85705
ALowenstein@xxx.net
520-555-1364 Cell • 520-555-7326 Home

GOAL

Environmental engineering position specializing in air and waste management.

BACKGROUND

- Engineer with experience in environmental regulatory analysis and research.
- Strong technical and communications skills.
- Familiarity with environmental regulatory programs.

RECENT PROJECTS

Research

- Development of experimental procedure for sampling and laboratory analysis of submicron aerosols using a serial filter and ion chromatography.
- Analysis of optical properties of aerosols using remote-sensing lidar signals.

Fieldwork

- Field inspection of underground disposal wells for compliance to EPA standards.
- Groundwater sampling at Superfund site.

RECENT PROJECTS *(continued)*

Technical Writing

- Creation of environmental impact statements.
- Development of sections of EPA reports to Congress.

EMPLOYERS

University of Arizona, Department of Atmospheric Sciences
Research Associate, 8/02 to Present

Richardson and Eastman Inc.
Environmental Researcher, 6/00 to 8/02

EDUCATION

B.S. in Environmental Engineering
University of Arizona, 2000

AFFILIATIONS

- Air and Waste Management Association
- American Society of Environmental Engineers

REFERENCES

Available on request.

A N D R E W   H I R A T A

6511 York Road * Tacoma, WA 98406

206-555-1861/Office * 206-555-3222/Home * A.Hirata@xxx.com

P R O F E S S I O N A L   R E G I S T E R E D   F O R E S T E R

OBJECTIVE

Seeking position as full-time industrial forester that will utilize my forestry skills and business administration ability.

JOB HISTORY

7/98 to Present: Senior Forester
Parkland Industries, Tacoma, WA

Duties: Responsible for all phases of procurement of timber from private landowners, including on-site inventories and appraisals; contract negotiations; subcontracting arrangements for tree removal; road layout; supervision of on-site workers; and direction of compliance with federal, state, and local environmental regulations.

6/96 to 7/98: Forester
Washington Resource Conservation Service, Seattle, WA

Duties: Team leader for regeneration projects. Responsible for site selection and preparation. Monitored growth, scheduled harvesting, inspected for disease, and treated as necessary.

EDUCATION

M.B.A.
University of Washington, Seattle, 1996

B.A. in Forestry
University of Washington, Seattle, 1991

Registered, State of Washington, Professional Forester
Designation

SKILLS

- Familiar with advanced photogrammetry and remote-sensing techniques.
- Experienced in use of measurement tools, including clinometer, increment borers, and bark gauges.
- Fluent in Spanish.

MEMBERSHIPS

- Society of American Foresters
- Society of Range Management

REFERENCES

On request.

Angela H. Stuart

3061 Fourth Street
Ellison Bay, Wisconsin 54210
a.stuart@xxx.com
414-555-7089

Objective

Opportunity to combine teaching and chemistry background in an
environmental education position.

Education

M.S. in Environmental Science, University of Wisconsin, Madison, 2000

Concentration: Chemistry

B.A. in Biology, University of Wisconsin, Madison, 1998

Minor: Education

Employment History

May 2004 to Present

Assistant Manager

Bancroft Center for Environmental Safety and Research

Current projects include development and implementation of laboratory safety
and hazardous materials management programs, documentation of compliance
with WDH and EPA regulations, creation of requests for proposals, and
evaluation of bids and grant proposals.

Employment History *(continued)*

July 2002 to May 2004

Activity Director

Riverdale Nature Center

Designed environmental activity/education programs for children and adults. Supervised volunteer staff of 10. Created educational materials and programs that integrate technology and nature for young visitors. Facilitated use of center by school and community groups.

July 2000 to July 2002

Assistant Educational Director

University of Wisconsin Museum of Natural History

Assisted museum director with development of educational materials, training of docents, and development of special workshops for students and staff. Assisted staff with course development and research projects as requested.

Skills

Proficient in use of Access, Excel, Word, Statgraf, and Cricket Graph.

Excellent lab skills, including experience preparing solutions and equipment for biochemistry laboratories.

Fluent in Spanish and Italian.

Memberships

National Education Association

North American Association for Environmental Education

References

Personal and professional references provided upon request.

BENJAMIN CROWELL

2900 South Driscoll Street
Atlanta, Georgia 30356
BJCrowell@xxx.com
(770) 555-6978 Work
(770) 555-5836 Home

EXPERIENCE

Independent Contractor—from 8/94 to Present

Recent Projects

- **American Packaging, Inc., Independent Systems Analyst**

Two-year contract. Responsibilities included development, specifications writing, modification of existing programs as necessary, and design and coding of new programs. Performed structural procedure testing. Responsible for data and program modifications, recompiling and rebinding, testing, and debugging.

- **GSI Chemical Corporation, Independent Programmer**

Assisted with setup of 30-member data processing department in Georgia branch office. Assignment included analyzing, coding, debugging, and implementing business applications, including payroll, general ledger, and inventory control. Implemented scientific applications, such as process modeling and engineering. Performed troubleshooting. Expanded and interconnected system hardware.

SKILLS

- Applications: SAP R/3, Siebel, Mathlab, Cable Billing, Crystal Reports, Benchmarks, Internet Security, Data Communications, Database Analyst, Device Drivers, Expert Systems, Embedded Systems, Inventory Control, Sales Analysis, EDI, Software Conversions and Systems Integration, Object Oriented Design and Programming, Asterisk

- Databases: Oracle 7/8i, DB2, SQL Server 7.0/2000, Access

SKILLS
continued

- Languages: C, C++, C#, Perl, Java2, J2EE, Python, PERL, Fortran 77, Visual Basic, Pick Basic, Cobol, UML, XML, XSL, X86 Assemblers

- Hardware and Operating Systems: Amdahl 580 (UTS 4.4), Apple Macintosh (OS 7 - 10.4), DEC Alpha (OpenVMS, OSF/1), HP 9000 (HP/UX 7.2 - 11.3), IBM 360 - z900 (VM, MVS - z390), IBM AS400 (OS/400), IBM RS6000 (AIX 3.2 - 4.3), IBM PC (Windows 2000, XP, Linux, and FreeBSD, VxWorks, QNX), Intel processors 80x86-Pentium 4, Motorola 680x0, PowerPC, SUN 220, 250, 4700, 10000 (Solaris 2.5 - 2.8)

- Protocols: RS232, RS449, V.35, Ethernet, SONET/SDH, Gigabit Ethernet, HDLC, LAPB (link layer X.25), Q.921, IBM BSC - 2780, 3270, 3780, 802.3, 802.4, 802.5, 802.11a/b/g, 802.14, 802.16, SDLC, X.25, Q.931, IGRP, EIGRP, OSPF, BGPv4, MPLS, RSVP, DOCSIS 1.1-2.0, ISDN, TCP/IP v4&v6, X.400, X.409, X.410, NFS, RFS, CMS Kermit, SNA, VTAM, CMS, RPC, HTML, JavaScript, VoIP, SMNP, SMTP, DNS, DHCP, CDMA, GSM, H.323, SIP

EDUCATION

B.S. in Computer Science, University of Virginia, 1994

REFERENCES

Available on request

carla mendez

8528 south fairfax street
dayton, ohio 45469
C.Mendez@xxx.com
513-555-5530 (cell)
513-555-5657 (home)

goal:

Transportation Safety Inspector II Position

overview:

Registered engineer with five years of civil engineering inspection experience with the Department of Transportation as a Safety Inspector I. Two years of experience in private sector working for a civil engineering firm specializing in hydrologic aspects of highway design and construction and design of wastewater treatment facilities.

employers:

Ohio Department of Transportation
Safety Inspector I
September 2001 to Present

Engineering Aide
Stevenson Industrial Design
August 1999 to September 2001

skills:

- AutoCAD drafting and design experience
- Thorough knowledge of Ohio Safety Inspection Code
- Strong communication skills
- High level of attention to detail in all written progress reports and safety inspection records

education:

Bachelor of Engineering, 1999
Ohio State University

affiliations:

- American Society of Civil Engineers
- Institute of Health Safety Professionals

references:

Available on request

MICHAEL REICHMANN

5343 S. Shore Dr.   Jacksonville, FL 32209
m.reichmann@xxx.com   (904) 555-4812

OBJECTIVE

Aerospace engineering position that would utilize my specialized chemistry skills

EMPLOYMENT

1999 to Present
Allerton Aviation, Inc., Jacksonville, FL
Aerospace Engineer

Conduct in-depth stress analysis of commercial aircraft engine components. Utilize hand and finite methods to assess structural integrity of core thrust reversers, compartment doors, and ducts. Check pressure loads for compliance with FAA standards. Consult closely with product development group to assure quality control during design phase.

1997 to 1999
Kussler Technology Group, Dallas, TX
Chemist

Directed research and development staff of six on project to develop adhesion modification of polycarbonate and composite aircraft transparency products. Tested polyarylates and polyester carbonates to find suitable outer ply and structural materials for commercial aircraft.

EDUCATION

B.S. from Purdue University, 1997
Double major: Aerospace Engineering, Chemistry

Proficient in use of Lotus 1-2-3 and FEM programs, including NASTRAN and PIPELINE

REFERENCES

Available on request

Allan Kusaka

4800 Breighton Street
Oakland, California 94609
*Allan.Kusaka@xxx.com * (415) 555-2837*

EDUCATION

M.S. in Public Health Administration
University of Hawaii

B.S. in Psychology
University of California, Berkeley

EXPERIENCE

General Manager
Oakland Medical Research Center
Oakland, California
2000 to Present

Direct day-to-day operations and long-range planning for medical research
center with annual budget of $2.5 million. Areas of responsibility include
financial planning, cost containment, and staffing.

Achievements

- Increased first-year profits by 10 percent
- Maintained steady financial growth
- Implemented marketing plan that resulted in 15 percent increase in
  contributions from private sector
- Instituted community outreach program to increase center's visibility

Assistant Research Director
Keystone Pharmaceutical, Inc.
San Francisco, California
1998 to 2000

Supervised pharmaceutical research studies into antidepressant medications.
Directed a research staff of 20 scientists.

Achievements

- Standardized lab procedures
- Introduced computer modeling system
- Reduced annual operating expenses by 5 percent

EXPERIENCE... continued

Assistant Administrator
Northwest Mental Health Center
Berkeley, California
1995 to 1998

Assisted general manager of 60-bed psychiatric center. Participated in all aspects of health management: educational, therapeutic, personnel. Involved in hiring and training of new staff members and volunteers. Assisted in direct patient care and emergency intervention as needed. Responsible for all billing.

Achievements

- Recruited and trained group of 14 new volunteers
- Secured a $250,000 federal grant for research in obsessive-compulsive disorders

AFFILIATIONS

- California Public Health Council
- American Management Association
- National Academy for Scientific Research

REFERENCES

Available upon request

Julie K. Hartley

894 Prescott Street

San Antonio, TX 78284

jhartley@xxx.com

Goal

Management of daily operation and long-range planning for environmental nonprofit group or professional association.

Abilities

- Financial Planning and Cost Containment
- Staffing

- Marketing
- Systems Analysis
- Grant Writing

Work Experience

Vice President
Western Natural Resources Council
San Antonio, TX
1999 to Present

Director of Marketing
Dallas Zoo
Dallas, TX
1997 to 1999

Membership Coordinator
Institute of Hazardous Materials Management
Denver, CO
1993 to 1997

Education

M.B.A. University of Texas   *B. S.* University of Texas
                                    Major: Biology
                                    Minor: Marketing

References

Available upon Request

Marcus Evans

442 Willow Road
Woodside, CA 94062
m.evans@xxx.com
213-555-6749

Goal

Entry-level technician position with a chemical or food-processing firm

Experience

University of California, Irvine, CA
Chemistry Lab Assistant, 1998 to Present

Assist with the management and maintenance of the graduate chemistry lab. Track inventory of chemicals and issue reorder requests. Assist student researchers with setup of lab equipment. Validate and record cost center codes for input into computer records system.

Woodside Community College, Woodside, CA
Math Tutor, 1994 to 1998

Assisted with setup of tutoring center. Screened and trained student tutors. Evaluated teaching materials. Maintained master schedule in Microsoft Outlook. Tutored students one on one and in groups. Reviewed exams and assignments to identify areas for improvement and develop learning strategies.

Woodside Public Library, Woodside, CA
Computer Center Volunteer, 1993 to 1995

Assisted library patrons with use of PCs, software, and Internet usage. Answered general questions and provided in-depth one-on-one training.

Education

B.S. in Chemistry, 1993
University of California, Irvine

References available on request

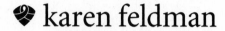 # karen feldman

*877 Chesterfield Street * Lincolnwood, IL 60646*
Karen.Feldman@xxx.com
(847) 555-9113

overview

Experienced systems programmer with background in consumer goods, telecommunications, and automotive industries.

technical knowledge

COBOL, IMS/DB, DBS, SQL, DB2, TERADATA, TESSERACT, CICS, FOCUS, SYMPHONY, PARADOX, VM/CMS, QMF, IMS, DB/DC, PASCAL, C++, SYQL, ORACLE

work record

Consultant to following companies, 1997 to present:

• New Age Organic Foods
• American Telecommunications
• Drexler Automotive Systems
• Southern Telecommunications Systems

achievements

New Age Organic Foods

• Successful implementation of new DataScan system for sales and marketing user group. System processed and converted information provided by Consumer Information Inc. and loaded it into TERADATA and DB2.
• Creation of new salary planning system using TESSERACT personnel management system in DB2 and CICS. Programs were written in COBOL II, CICS, with embedded SQL.
• Conversion of accounts receivable system into MSA format. Interfaces were written in COBOL under MVS/XA.

achievements, *continued*

American Telecommunications

- Development of new billing system based on DB2.
- Development of production applications using COBOL, CICS, and embedded SQL.
- Creation of ad hoc reports using QMF and SQL.

Drexler Automotive Systems

- Timely and competent completion of inventory, order entry, and conversion projects.
- Successful completion of supervisor training program.
- Service as assistant quality control supervisor.
- Successful supervision of online inspectors, under direction of Quality Control Supervisor.

Southern Telecommunications Systems

- Successful development of fixed assets systems for newly formed corporate division.
- Creation of online manufacturing tracking and inventory control system.
- Design and implementation of new telephone invoking system incorporating PC-to-mainframe interaction.

education

B.S., Computer Science

Northern Illinois University, 1997

references

Personal and professional references available and forwarded upon request.

Monica Bradley

1221 Lindquist Road
Los Angeles, CA 98432
Cell: 907-555-8751
E-mail: M.Bradley@xxx.net

--- **Experience** ---

Background in city planning, home inspection, building trades, and project management.

--- **Work History** ---

March 1999 to Present   **City of Los Angeles**   **Zoning Commissioner**
Manage all aspects of zoning and urban planning for the city. Facilitate zoning meetings, review building requests from new businesses, make recommendations to mayor's office, issue zoning permits. Coordinate with Department of Community Development on long-term planning issues. Supervise staff of four.

June 1997 to March 1999   **Best Home Services**   **Home Inspector**
Conducted on-site inspections of new and previously owned homes for buyers. Investigated structural integrity of properties; tested appliances, heating and cooling systems, and water pressure. Issued written reports of property status, including suggestions for repairs as needed.

--- **Training** ---

Completed three-year apprenticeship in building trades sponsored by Ryerson Technical Institute. Coursework included carpentry, business management, and home inspection.

Member, International Conference of Building Inspectors (ICBO)

Certified Building Inspector, State of Illinois

References Available

William Newberry

988 South Parker Road
Houston, Texas 77386
Cell: (713) 555-1947
E-mail: Bill.Newberry@xxx.com

Overview

Commercial applications programmer familiar with large operating environments, database management, direct access technologies, and remote processing. Some exposure to CRT drivers, virtual systems, and database handlers.

Skills

COBOL, BASIC, RPG II, Pascal, C, C++, SYQL, ORACLE

Job Responsibilities

- Program design
- Coding
- Systems testing and debugging
- Creation of program documentation

Employment

Houston Savings & Loan, Houston
Programmer/Analyst, June 1995 to Present

Security Insurance, Dallas
Systems Analyst, May 1991 to June 1995

S & J Manufacturing, Dallas
Programmer, April 1987 to May 1991

Education

B.S., Baylor University, 1987
Major: Computer Science
Minor: Accounting

References Available

Jason Rodriquez

6547 Whitetail Lane
Galveston, NM 77550
Cell: 409-566-7493
E-mail: j.rodriquez@xxx.com

Status

- Independent consultant specializing in Web publishing and collaboration tools and online communities.
- Thorough knowledge of Web standards, e-mail, and other Internet protocols, as well as skilled Linux system administration.

Education

B.Sc. with specialization in Computing Science
University of Texas, Austin, TX
December 1995

Experience

September 1997 - present
Systems Programmer
World Wide Web Consortium (W3C), MIT/CSAIL, Austin, TX

- Maintain the computing infrastructure of a busy, high-profile research group, including their Web servers, e-mail systems, mailing lists, user accounts, and publishing tools.
- Responsibilities include Linux system administration, backups, security, network administration, tool development, user support.
- Created the W3C HTML Validation Service.
- Work daily with staff and collaborators who are distributed around the world.

Experience *continued*

April 1996 - July 1997
WWW Programmer/Analyst
Office of the Registrar and Student Awards, University of Texas

- Provided advice and guidance to the office on all Web-related issues.
- Designed, created, and administered online application forms for students, staff, and faculty (example: Application for Undergraduate Admission).
- Liaised with other campus and government-related organizations on the technical aspects of collaborative Web projects.
- Administered the office's Web server (running Apache on Linux).

Skills

- Experience with various Unix systems, including Linux, Solaris, SunOS, AIX, IRIX, BSD/OS, FreeBSD, and others; also over 10 years of experience as a full-time Unix system administrator.
- Experience running Apache-like Web servers, maintaining servers with millions of documents serving tens of millions of hits per day.
- Extensive Web application programming experience, including text search software, database interfaces, interactive games, and interfaces to large data archives.
- Extremely thorough knowledge of the Internet, including Web standards, e-mail and other Internet protocols, open source software, and online communities.
- Thorough knowledge of Unix shell utilities, Perl, and automation in a Unix environment.

References available on request.

Jade Ishida

733 Stevens Road

Des Plaines, IL 60016

(847) 555-6123 Home

(847) 555-8127 Cell

Goal

Management position in counseling/psychology with university hospital system or private treatment facility.

Expertise

- Psychological counseling experience in both hospital and clinic settings. Member of multidisciplinary rehabilitation team for patients with spinal cord injuries. Director of hospital and outpatient mental health programs.
- Teaching and curriculum development experience at the university level.
- Ongoing clinical research analyzing the effect of behavior modification techniques on substance abuse.

Employment

2001 to Present
Assistant Professor, Psychology Department
Elmhurst College

Teach Abnormal Psychology, Child Psychology, and Research Methods. Supervise nursing, psychology, and premed students in on-site psychology clinical rotations. Conduct research. Provide input into department's ongoing curriculum development.

Employment

continued

1998 to 2001
Director, Psychosocial Services
Midwest Rehabilitation Institute

Supervised staff of 10 counselors and social work professionals at rehabilitation institute providing comprehensive care for patients recovering from spinal cord injuries. Developed care plans in conjunction with medical, occupational therapy, and physical therapy professionals. Responsible for staff scheduling, evaluations, in-service presentations, patient education, and discharge planning.

1996 to 1998
Director
Ridgeway Treatment Center

Managed outpatient substance abuse program serving patients in transition from inpatient to outpatient care. Supervised staff and developed treatment programs. Directed community education and outreach efforts.

Credentials

M.S. in Psychology
University of Illinois, 1996

B.S.
Northern Illinois University, 1994
Major: Psychology; Minor: Business

Member, American Psychiatric Association

References

Available

TYRELL WRIGHT

● ● ● ● ●

3215 Cunningham Road
Boston, MA 02151
Tyrell.Wright@xxx.com
617-555-3498

● WORK HISTORY ●

2000 to Present
Harrison Technical Institute
Director, Metalworking Division

● Direct metalworking department at vocational school with
current enrollment of 800 students.

● Hire, train, and supervise staff teaching tool-and-die making,
welding, and automotive mechanics courses.

● Develop curriculum in conjunction with school officials and local
trade union.

1992 to 2000
TRS Metalworks Inc.
Tool Programmer

● Used knowledge of machining operations, metals, blueprints,
and machine programming to write programs for CNC tool-and-
die machines.

● Trained machinists and tool-and-die makers in use of state-of-the-
art CNC software programs.

Page 1 of 2

● WORK HISTORY ●
CONTINUED

1990 to 1992
Remington Industries, Inc.
Tool Design Consultant

- Specialized in large-scale industrial construction.
- Responsible for cost estimating, equipment purchase, software programming, and staff training.

● CREDENTIALS ●

A.S., Northwest Technical College, 1990

● ● ● ● ●

REFERENCES AVAILABLE

Sample Cover Letters

This chapter contains sample cover letters for people pursuing a wide variety of jobs and careers in science.

There are many different styles of cover letters in terms of layout, level of formality, and presentation of information. These samples also represent people with varying amounts of education and work experience. Choose one cover letter or borrow elements from several different cover letters to help you construct your own.

CARLOS DE LA PAZ

9916 Pasco Drive

Pullman, WA 99164

(509) 555-5616

June 17, 20__

Ms. Barbara Conheady, Personnel Director
State of Washington, Environmental Services Division
567 North Fetzer Street
Pullman, WA 99164

Dear Ms. Conheady:

Enclosed is an updated copy of my resume for your files. I hope that you will keep me in mind for any Vector Control Supervisor positions that open up this year. As you know, I can offer the following skills:

• Pest control experience gained as Vector Control Worker II with the state of Washington
• Current mosquito abatement experience
• Safe operation of power sprayers, trucks, spreaders, and tractors
• Valid license and clean driving record

I hope to continue to progress in my career with the state of Washington and will call you before the end of the month to discuss any possible job openings. If you wish to contact me before then, my home number is (509) 555-5616.

Thank you for your time and consideration.

Sincerely,

Carlos De la Paz

Jane Kingston, Ph.D.

961 Alton Street
Bethesda, MD 20014
(301) 555-2908
Jane.Kingston@xxx.com

June 13, 20___

Mr. Patrick Brenden, Director
Search Committee
National Center for Ocean Sciences Research
988 Shore Road
St. Augustine, FL 32085

Dear Mr. Brenden:

The enclosed resume explains in detail my qualifications for the Director of Research position you recently advertised in the *Journal of Marine Sciences*.

My background includes an M.S. in Oceanography and five years of experience in the administration of research and development projects. My current responsibilities as Research Administrator for the National Institute of Marine Biology include screening research proposals and developing and implementing technical standards and program objectives.

In addition to the specific abilities and job experience listed on my resume, I have strong supervisory and teaching skills, effective written and oral communication skills, and a high degree of commitment to my work.

I am available at your convenience if you wish to arrange an interview.

Sincerely,

Jane Kingston

Jacob Harvey

486 Carmel Road ❖ Anaheim, California 92803
(714) 555-6976 ❖ j.harvey@xxx.com

July 11, 20__

Ms. Alicia Weston, Director
Anaheim Wildlife Center
845 Mission Street
Anaheim, California 92803

Dear Ms. Weston:

I enjoyed your recent lecture on preserving Mono Lake and greatly admire the work you are doing to preserve the habitat of California gulls and black-necked grebes. It was a privilege to have you at the zoo and to learn more about your organization.

Following the lecture, you indicated that you may be adding new staff positions soon. I would certainly like to be considered for any appropriate positions that open up. Enclosed is a copy of my resume, which explains my work at Anaheim Children's Zoo. I would be glad to provide further information in person or by phone if you have any questions.

Thank you again for your informative lecture. I hope we meet again soon.

Sincerely,

Jacob Harvey

Miles Edmonds

5328 Jefferson Street

St. Louis, MO 63119

m.edmonds@xxx.com

314-555-0598 - Home

314-555-0597 - Cell

May 16, 20__

Mr. Carl Edelfelt, President

Edelfelt Environmental Testing Services

8784 Scott Street

Palo Alto, CA 94304

Dear Mr. Edelfelt:

I recently learned from the vice president of your company, Susan Satterfield, of your need for an air quality electronics technician. I hope you will agree that my skills and experience match your firm's current needs.

As my resume indicates, I am currently an air quality electronics technician for the state of Missouri. Although I enjoy my current job, I am always looking for an opportunity for professional growth. I am also willing to relocate.

I will be in Palo Alto from May 20 to May 27. Would it be possible to arrange an interview during that time? I will call your office early next week to make arrangements.

Thank you for considering my credentials.

Sincerely,

Miles Edmonds

Carolyn Haynes

826 Morris Road
East Lansing, MI 48826
Home: 517-555-1810
Cell: 517-555-3812

Ms. Darcy Hanson
Personnel Director
Food World Corporation
8922 Gleason Street
East Lansing, MI 48824

February 23, 20__

Dear Ms. Hanson:

I was pleased to see your online ad for an assistant research scientist on Food World's website. My experience as a quality control tester for IGN Foodservice Inc. has given me the skills you currently require:

- Knowledge of FDA quality control standards
- Understanding of quality control testing methods and procedures
- Interest in the field of food formulation/product development

Before taking my current position at IGN, I worked for a gourmet food distributor operating both a retail outlet and a mail-order business. This experience gave me insight into consumer preferences for products and packaging that would be useful in new product development.

As you can see, Ms. Hanson, I have the skills that would enable me to excel as your new assistant research scientist.

Please feel free to call or e-mail me with any questions you may have or to set up a time to meet. I appreciate your consideration and look forward to the possibility of joining your staff.

Sincerely,

Carolyn Haynes

To: **FRANK PETERSON, HUMAN RESOURCES DIRECTOR**
Kepler Pharmaceutical
9810 Arch Street
Kalamazoo, MI 46302

From: **DEBORAH HERMANN**
529 Washington Street
Kalamazoo, MI 46302
614-555-7523

Date: May 2, 20___

Re: SUMMER EMPLOYMENT

Is Kepler Pharmaceutical in need of laboratory assistants again this summer? If so, I would like to be considered for a position. As you know, I worked in the research lab last summer, supervised by Carol Jones.

I gained further experience this year as a laboratory assistant in the chemistry lab at Western Michigan University. My duties in the lab included scheduling research projects, preparing media and solutions, and conducting supply and chemical inventories. I hope to continue to build my skills by finding a lab assistant position this summer.

I will call next week to find out if I can assist your company again this summer. Thanks for your consideration, Mr. Peterson. If you would like to speak to me before then, please e-mail me at D.Hermann@xxx.com

Sincerely,

Debbie Hermann

A N D R E W   H I R A T A

6511 York Road * Tacoma, WA 98406

206-555-1861/Office * 206-555-3222/Home * A.Hirata@xxx.com

P R O F E S S I O N A L   R E G I S T E R E D   F O R E S T E R

May 23, 20__

Mr. Vance D. Boyd, Vice President
Corrigan Land Management, Inc.
109 South Brockton Road
Tacoma, WA 98406

Dear Mr. Boyd:

I enjoyed our telephone conversation Tuesday morning. Thanks for taking the time to discuss the contract administrator position.

Enclosed is the resume you requested; it provides the details of my work experience and educational background. As I mentioned during our conversation, contract negotiations are an important aspect of my job at Parkland Industries, one at which I excel and enjoy. I would be pleased to apply my skills to the position of contract administrator at Corrigan and feel confident that I would be a great fit for the position.

I am available at your convenience should you wish to schedule an interview. I am most easily reached during the morning, as I often schedule visits to job sites during the afternoons.

Thank you again for your time.

Sincerely,

Andrew Hirata

George Hale

416 Whitworth Avenue

East Hampton, NY 11937

---

(631) 555-2846

July 21, 20__

Mr. David Torneau
Human Resources Manager
ETS Manufacturing
413 Barrington Road
Nutley, NJ 07110

Dear Mr. Torneau:

One of your current employees, Jason Howard, recently informed me that
ETS Manufacturing is in need of a dedicated entry-level chemist.

I recently graduated from Bennington College, where I was a teaching assistant in the Chemistry Department. In addition, I spent last summer working
as a laboratory technician in the plastics division of Moser Manufacturing. My
goal is to specialize in polymer chemistry, and I hope that I can begin to pursue that goal at ETS.

Jason speaks highly of the company, and I would love the chance to join ETS
Manufacturing. Please let me know of any openings, current or future. I
appreciate your consideration and will stay in touch.

Sincerely,

George Hale
G.Hale@xxx.com

JAY ALLEN

611 Trenton Road ✦ Sacramento, CA 95819
jay.allen@xxx.com ✦ (916) 555-9861

October 13, 20__

Ms. Ramona Hartz, Director of Research
Environmental Resources Council
8813 Meade Road
Sacramento, CA 95819

Dear Ms. Hartz:

I learned of your need for a statistician from your online newsletter, and I wish to
apply for the position.

My current job with the state's soil conservation service involves compiling
statistics on soil erosion, monitoring data, and preparing written status reports for
the agency's director.

My preparation for your position includes a degree in Environmental Studies from
the University of California at San Diego. My minor was Statistics.

Please take a moment to review the enclosed resume, which explains my
professional qualifications in greater detail. You can call me at (916) 555-9861 or e-
mail me at jay.allen@xxx.com to arrange for an interview.

I look forward to hearing from you.

Sincerely,

Jay Allen
611 Trenton Road
Sacramento, CA 95819

Martin T. Vasquez

632 Delaney Road
Monterey, CA 93942
M.Vasquez@xxx.com
(831) 555-0797

. . . .

May 4, 20___

Ms. Paula West, Director
Monterey Botanical Gardens
9821 Westfield Court
Monterey, CA 93940

Dear Ms. West:

Kevin Lessing recently gave me your name because he is aware of my search for an entry-level botanist position. I currently work at Lessing Nursery and have been assisting Mr. Lessing in the research and development of orchid hybrids.

The enclosed resume explains my work at Lessing Nursery and summarizes my relevant coursework at Harrison College.

I will receive my B.S. in Botany from Harrison next month, and I hope to find an entry-level position as a botanist following graduation. I would appreciate knowing of any openings at Monterey Botanical Gardens. I would also welcome any advice you have to offer on securing a job in your field.

I appreciate your guidance and look forward to the possibility of working with you.

Yours truly,

Martin T. Vasquez

P.S. Mr. Lessing sends his warmest regards.

PARADISE PEST CONTROL

9618 Bishop Street
Lihue, HI 96766
kevin.hutchins@xxx.net
(808) 555-6712 Work
(808) 555-9836 Home

January 16, 20___

Mr. Paul Cook, Owner
Cook Construction
654 Mei Road
Kalaheo, HI 96740

Dear Mr. Cook:

Thank you for calling Paradise Pest Control this morning to discuss preconstruction treatment for your ongoing construction projects. As you suggested, I will be happy to tour the construction sites with you in the near future to determine how best to meet your needs at each site. But first, let me provide you with more information about Paradise Pest Control and my own credentials.

Paradise Pest Control was established in 1994 and enjoys an excellent reputation in the local community. We offer a wide range of services, including general pest control, termite inspection, ground termite control, tent fumigation, preconstruction treatment, and escrow clearance. As the enclosed resume indicates, I had extensive experience in the field before opening my own business. I would be pleased to provide a list of references, including current clients, if you wish.

I feel confident that Paradise Pest Control can supply the quality of preconstruction treatment you're seeking, and I look forward to meeting with you to discuss options. Please call me at either of the numbers above to schedule an appointment.

Sincerely,

Kevin Hutchins, Owner

Scott Parker

327 Maple Street
Aspen, CO 81612
S.Parker@xxx.com
970-555-0599

—⁓—

June 16, 20__

Ms. Sharon Grant, Director
Northwest Expeditions
453 Park Street
Aspen, CO 81612

Dear Ms. Grant:

The enclosed resume provides a brief overview of my qualifications for the tour guide position you recently advertised in the *Denver Post*. Please note that I am available for local tours or work abroad. I speak fluent Spanish, have a B.S. in Geology, and have traveled extensively in South America.

My salary requirements are negotiable, and I am willing to work a flexible schedule. Most important, my varied skills and my enthusiasm as a hiker, rafter, and guide would make me a valuable addition to your staff.

I would be pleased to explain my credentials and discuss your current needs in person.

Sincerely,

Scott Parker

Angela H. Stuart

3061 Fourth Street
Ellison Bay, Wisconsin 54210
a.stuart@xxx.com
414-555-7089

September 19, 20__

Ms. Elizabeth Cook, Director
Carabelle Children's Museum
3200 South Santa Rosa Street
Carabelle, Florida 32322

Dear Ms. Cook:

I discovered your museum on a recent trip to Carabelle and admired the natural
history and science exhibits as well as the nature trail and pioneer village. You and
your staff have done an excellent job of creating a place where children can learn
about Florida's environment and about environmental science in general.

I am currently seeking an opportunity to put my skills in chemistry and environmental
education to work for an organization such as yours. I would be grateful if you would
take a moment to review the enclosed resume. As it indicates, I have a proven record
of developing quality educational materials and programs in various academic,
nonprofit, and corporate settings.

If no appropriate positions are currently available, please keep my resume for future
reference. Thank you for your consideration and for the enjoyable afternoon I spent at
the Carabelle Children's Museum.

Sincerely,

Angela H. Stuart

SUSAN WRIGHT

657 King Court
Atlanta, Georgia 30356
Susan.Wright@xxx.com
404-555-4959

August 14, 20__

Mr. Paul Hyde, President
Southwest Environmental Testing Inc.
4079 Sanford Street
Atlanta, Georgia 30356

Dear Mr. Hyde:

Thank you for taking time to review the enclosed resume, which explains my environmental engineering qualifications. I am looking for an opportunity with an environmental firm such as yours where I can use my knowledge of environmental testing in field work and in project management.

I recently moved to Atlanta from West Virginia, where I was employed by Powell Metallurgical as a quality control engineer. My job involved management of meteorological and particulate monitoring programs for mining operations. Through collection and processing of data sets, I ensured the company's compliance with EPA and state guidelines for pollution control.

I work equally well alone or as part of a team, and I feel that I would be an asset to your organization. My prior work experience and B.S. in Environmental Engineering from the University of Florida have prepared me to meet a variety of challenges in environmental engineering, including air pollution control design, wastewater system design, and atmospheric dispersion modeling.

I would appreciate learning of any openings on your staff that require these skills. I will look forward to hearing how I can assist Southwest Environmental Testing.

Sincerely,

Susan Wright

ADBAR JALIL

661 S. Weston Rd.

Denver, CO 80203

adbar.jalil@xxx.com

303-555-4059

June 23, 20___

ATTN: Walter Lipsky, Director
        Denver National Weather Service
        6218 Wilcox Street
        Denver, CO 80209

Do you ever wish for additional staff during meteorological emergencies? Are your organization's long-term goals and research projects uncompleted because of your heavy workload? If so, please consider my credentials.

I have extensive experience in atmospheric science research and currently do research for the University of Colorado, where I have taught undergraduate courses in Meteorology.

I am available on a contract or hourly consulting basis; in addition, I am willing to consider full- or part-time employment with your organization.

If the Weather Service has any additional staffing needs, please feel free to contact me via phone or e-mail to set up a time to meet. Thanks for your time and consideration.

Sincerely,

Adbar Jalil

ALICIA ALVEREZ

144 South Prospect Street, Tucson, Arizona 85705
a.alverez@xxx.com
Home (520) 555-7348
Office (520) 555-7939

March 16, 20__

Mr. Eric Orstan, President
Eco-Tek Systems
9840 Hartman Street
Charlotte, North Carolina 28213

Dear Mr. Orstan:

I will be moving to Charlotte this summer and am seeking a position with an environmental or civil engineering firm. Is your firm in need of someone with a strong background in wastewater engineering?

I have extensive experience in the design of wastewater treatment facilities. My current employer values my skills in computer modeling and simulation as well as my knowledge of EPA and state and federal environmental regulations. Perhaps I can put these same skills to work for Eco-Tek.

I will be in Charlotte early next month and would enjoy meeting you to discuss employment opportunities. I will call next week to inquire about scheduling an appointment.

Meanwhile, thank you for your consideration.

Sincerely,

Alicia Alverez

Margaret Chapman

9484 N. Ellis St., Baltimore, MD 21203

maggie.chapman@xxx.com

410-555-3949 - Home

410-555-5902 - Cell

April 22, 20__

Mr. George Schonfeld
Senior Editor
Academic Press
Garden City, NY 11430

Dear Mr. Schonfeld:

Please accept the enclosed resume in response to your call for editors that appeared in the April issue of *Publishers Weekly*. I have 10 years of experience as an editor and technical writer preparing publications and proposals for the scientific community.

My current position involves both production and acquisitions editing. It demands the same qualities you seek: strong organizational skills, the ability to work well under pressure, and respect for deadlines.

I am familiar with your publications and admire the high editorial standard you set for your books. It would be a pleasure to assist you.

Please let me know if you need further information to evaluate my credentials. I would be happy to supply references and/or writing samples.

I look forward to hearing from you when you are further along in the selection process.

Sincerely,

Margaret Chapman

KEN SUMNER

17 Market Street
Guilford, CT 06437
(203) 555-0805/Office
(203) 555-8532/Home

May 9, 20__

Ms. Sylvia Ebener, Director of Personnel
Guilford County Agricultural Office
632 Third Street
Guilford, CT 06437

Dear Ms. Ebener:

This Sunday's *Guilford Gazette* announced that you are seeking candidates for the position of Agricultural Chemicals Inspector II. Please review the enclosed application, which details my qualifications for the job.

As my resume indicates, I have worked as a health inspector for the state of Vermont, as a commodity grader for the U.S. Department of Agriculture, and as a quality control manager in the private sector.

My background and skills seem ideally suited to your current needs: I understand FDA and state consumer health and safety regulations, have strong analytical and communications skills, and am willing to travel.

I am available at your convenience to meet and discuss my qualifications further. I am most easily reached at my office in the early morning or by e-mail at K.Sumner@xxx.com.

I look forward to hearing from you.

Sincerely,

Ken Sumner

Jed Carrera

5 Mason Road
Lincoln, UT 84074
(435) 555-2974

July 19, 20__

Mr. Patrick Kendrickson, Vice President
Midwest Harvestors
P.O. Box 169
Nauvoo, IL 62354

Dear Mr. Kendrickson:

Your recent advertisement in *AgriBusiness* for a soil scientist drew my attention. My work with the state of Utah involves many of the duties you describe. As an Agricultural Scientist II, I am responsible for conducting soil surveys, determining proper crop rotation and land use, and assessing the overall health of crops. I am proud to say that I've been able to assist the state of Utah in developing extremely healthy, pest-resistant agricultural products.

Before moving to Utah in 1995, I was a research assistant at my alma mater, Florida State. I am sure that my research there, analyzing frost tolerance, could be put to good use at Midwest Harvestors.

I will be in Illinois most of August visiting family and would like to schedule an interview. I appreciate your consideration and look forward to hearing from you.

Sincerely,

Jed Carrera

TO: **Roger Best, Director of Personnel**
        Ohio Department of Transportation
        921 S. Merrill St.
        Dayton, OH 45469

FROM: **Carla Morris**
        Safety Inspection Division
        8528 S. Fairfax St.
        Dayton, OH 45469

DATE: May 8, 20__

RE: *Application for Transportation Safety Inspector II Position*

———————————

Thank you for taking time this morning to explain the application process for the Safety Inspector II position. Enclosed are my resume and application.

I understand that after the committee reviews all promotion requests, I will be notified by mail regarding its decision.

I appreciate being considered for promotion and am excited about the prospect of assuming greater responsibility here at the Department of Transportation.

Should you have any questions regarding my qualifications, please let me know. I am most often in my office (extension 433) during the afternoons from 1:00 to 5:00.

Regards,

Carla Morris